Susan Wenger

The Port-Wine Sea

A PARODY

AmErica House
BALTIMORE

The cover and frontispiece were drawn by Jon Pearson, an extra-ordinarily effective speaker, artist, thinking skills consultant, and author of "Drawing on the Inventive Mind."

The author is grateful to Jon for his pictures and his moral support, and also thanks Sarah Taylor Jones and Matthew Turco for help in getting the musical inserts into computerized format.

First printing

Library of Congress Catalog Card Number: 98-83015

ISBN: 1-893162-00-1
PUBLISHED BY AMERICA HOUSE BOOK PUBLISHERS
www.ericahouse.com
Baltimore

Printed in the United States of America

Dedication: with gratitude to Patrick O'Brian for so many hours of joy; to midshipman Erika and to midshipman Whimsy, and of course, to Win (which he was made post in '68, and neither of us is flying the blue peter yet, neither).

For what do we live, but to make sport for our neighbors, and laugh at them in our turn?
- *Jane Austen*

What is history but a fable agreed upon?
- *Napoleon Bonaparte*

A strong nor-wester's blowing, Bill,

Hark! Don't ye hear it roar, now?

Lord help 'em, how I pities all

Unhappy folks on shore now!

- William Pitt

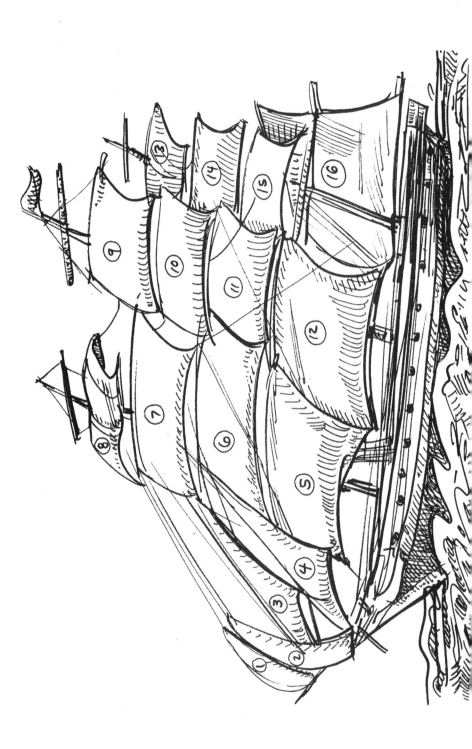

The sails of a rigged ship, hung out to dry as usual.

1 A sail, of course	9 A sail, of course
2 A sail, of course	10 A sail, of course
3 A sail, of course	11 A sail, of course
4 A sail, of course	12 A sail, of course
5 A sail, of course	13 A sail, of course
6 A sail, of course	14 A sail, of course
7 A sail, of course	15 A sail, of course
8 A sail, of course	16 A sail, of course

1

The music-room in the Admiral's home, a tall, note-filled, pillared orthotetrakaidecahedral canyon, was filled with the triumphant first movement of Locatelli's long-lost C major quartet (*Sacramenta di Primavera*); the manuscript having been found only recently in a large old garret in Rome. The players, clad in black suits with tails and yellow bow-ties, were playing with passion as they visualized a postlude group concert with the admiral's wife after the guests had departed. And on the little gilt chairs, at least one of the audience was visualizing with equal intensity, bobbing on his creaky chair in time with his own private passion. He was a large, sudoriferous man, at least seventeen stone, with long, oft-flowing yellow hair, worn clubbed behind in the naval fashion, not cut in the modern Brutus or Croppie fashion. He was wearing his best uniform for his anticipated tryst with Mrs. Tarte—the white-lapelled blue coat (with traces of suet pudding studding downward very like buttons), a white waistcoat, similarly stippled with food stains despite having been scrubbed clean by his steward that very morning, heavy double-gilt epaulettes, the red ribbon of the Bath across his broad chest, the Webelo aquanaut badge on his lapel, and the silver medal of the Nile in his buttonhole. His number one scraper, resting on his knee and bobbing in time with his passion, was adorned with a grotesque, garish ornament—huge rhinestones shaped in a spray, with a wind-up music box mechanism that played, "The Roast Beef of Old England."

On the small gilt chair next to his dozed his particular friend—physician/espionage agent Stephen Nattering, a rum-looking cove, an ill-kempt, dirty-faced man, with a pallid face and a more pallid, close-cropped skull, which showed through where his wig, poorly tied by a slipknot under his chin, had slipped awry. His mouth was agape, showing mottled teeth; he was deep in an opium-induced slumber. As the notes of the quartet rose in pitch, so did the old doctor's snores, to the point where the sailor was quite embarrassed by the stares of his hostess, Molly Tarte.

As the players smoothly closed the gentle andante of the piece, the two violins and the 'cello suddenly opened on a unison statement of the five-note declarative which launches the Allegro con Finale (the famous poom-poom-poom-poom-poom segment).

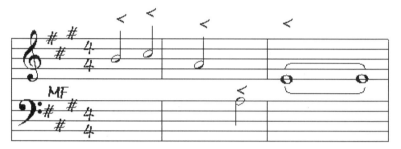

The viola and the 'cello then carried the same five notes into the lower registers of both instruments with the same emphasis and slow deliberation, then began arguing over the same five notes with different timings, pitches and emphases, commencing a spirited fugue but carefully avoiding an ostinati, which would have allowed the violins the weather gauge back into the main action. All the higher strings could manage was an occasional chirp or a pizzicato embellishment atop the more profound entanglements from below. This extraordinary state of affairs continued for some moments while, oblivious to all, Nattering snored away, to the naval captain's growing humiliation.

A discreet nudge would not serve, would not do at all. He drove his elbow into the old man's ribs with a ferocity that was savage even by royal naval standards. Stephen flew off the gilt chair, crashing violently into the 'cello, smashing it entirely into smithereens.

"Jesus, Joseph and Mary," he exclaimed loudly. "I was quite dreaming that I was lying alongside me dearly beloved wife Diana, and that blow to my ribs was <u>exactly</u> the way she strikes me... By all the saints... " His voice trailed off as he realized where he was, and he slowly regained his feet, apologizing to the musician for the destruction of his instrument, and slunk back to his now quite upturned chair, his cold, reptilian eyes fixed upon the innocent "who, me?" countenance of his friend.

Jack Audibly sighed happily and turned to the doctor with a benign smile. He never acted out of malice, and his natural good humor rose to the fore at once. "Was you asleep, brother?" he asked cheerfully. "You missed a prodigious good note, if you was sleeping. There's nothing like the smashing of an old 'cello for ending a swelling crescendo."

The trio ended abruptly, the cellist staring at the bridge of his 'cello, the only part to have survived, and the musicians gazing in astonishment at the shining shards of polished hardwood that were all that remained of the 'cello. They glared right hard at the unfortunate cellist, a lanky young man with a put-upon air and bad skin, apprehensive about the destruction of his instrument and wondering if his father would buy him another; this being the second one he'd had smashed up this week; but none of the players accused him of malfeasance aloud. Mrs. Tarte, the admiral's wife, took the floor and assailed her harp into a long and apparently technically difficult piece. Gazing upon her as she straddled her instrument, Jack Audibly felt his love of music rise again, partially concealed by his scraper. His mind wandered to his unhappy situation: no ship, no promise of a ship, no future. The war was clearly winding down; the madman Napoleon was pinned and penned, and there were more naval captains than there were ships to be captained. His attempt to rig the stock exchange had been foiled, and the money he had invested in the endeavor was quite gone. He sighed. Notes were due, and notes with which to pay them were in short supply.

Molly Tarte, misinterpreting entirely his sigh, quickly drew her piece to the close, and the audience rose good-naturedly and applauded their hostess. She curtseyed low, displaying an ample bosom surrounded by blue-white pearls given to her by Jack

Audibly. The audience applauded louder; she curtseyed lower. Captain Audibly rose to his feet with painful difficulty, and clapped quite loudly.

Molly was not to be available to him that evening. Admiral Tarte stood by her side, glaring angrily at the assembled throng, and they slowly dissipated under his fierce eye. The musicians cased their instruments regretfully and drifted out. Jack Audibly resisted his strong inclination to beat the admiral down with his little gilt chair, and merely waved his hand and left the room. He took brandy with the admiral in the small library, dissatisfied with himself and the situation, but unable to pursue the chase at this juncture in time. They talked not at all of music, or of cuckoldry, or of the choir of magpies in the lemon-trees outside, but of the various ships of the line they were so intimately familiar with, and of the men who commanded them, and of the men who served the men who commanded them. Eventually, the admiral yawned and stood, and Captain Audibly took his leave and fled the debacle, returning at a brisk pace to the room he shared with Nattering at the Clown Inn.

It was not a dark and stormy night, no shots rang out, no maids screamed, no pirate ships (i.e. British frigates) appeared upon the horizon. Yet scudding clouds covered the gibbous moon more often than not. Some of the clouds elsewhere in the sky caught enough light from the moon to cast a wan surreality over the street; an effect that was augmented by wisps of fog curling around the corners. Down the street, a momentary glimmer of moonlight shone on roof tiles before that area was again cast into obscurity. Almost overhead on a treetop, a hunched figure and the gleam of a large eye betrayed the position of an owl. The operculum on its ear twitched; the owl spotted Audibly, screeched in tones no man had ever heard before, swiveling its head to stare at him, and in its abject terror, plummeted from the tree like a landlubber from a foretopsail, bouncing once from a branch before crashing at Jack's feet, a lone feather floating past Jack's nose as the owl's huge night eyes clouded, dimmed, closed for the last time.

His attention was caught by a sleepy-eyed rider, cantering homeward. The horse stared suspiciously at Jack, his numinous eyes slowly widening in fear. Jack stared back for a few seconds, then backed away placatingly. The horse whined, moaned, and abruptly reared, throwing his rider. Jack stared in amazement. He started to the rider's assistance. The horse emitted an almost human scream, whipped his tail around and fled; the rider rubbed his head and glared angrily towards Jack, but stopped in his tracks at the sight of the ribbons and bows, flashes, epaulettes, clanking medals, gold hoop earrings, multi-buckled castineted flamenco boots, spats and chelengks.

"How odd," Captain Audibly thought to himself. Like a true Royal Naval officer, he felt more curiosity than remorse for the deaths caused by his passage. He took a fish from the pocket of his boatcloak and munched it as he continued in his path, inwardly pleased that Stephen Nattering had not observed the event; Stephen surely would have delivered a homily about institutional memory in animals, or some petty jest about horse sense. A small squirrel or rat peered at him, chuttered nervously, and ran, ran.

The Clown was a shabby, run-down inn, smelling of spilled beer and long-dead fish, but it did boast a dusky peach of a chambermaid in Mercedes-Benz. Jack Audibly was not in a mood to enjoy her tonight, however; his mind dwelling on his financial difficulties and how he would explain to his dear wife, Sophie, that he had spent all his prize money on stocking his wine cabinet, and they wouldn't be able to lay a kitchen floor this year. He passed Mercedes-Benz absent-mindedly, pausing only briefly to crush the breath out of her sweet, plump, supple, almond-smelling bosom, and turned into his room. Nattering wasn't in, but that did not surprise Captain Audibly in the slightest. "He probably stopped to admire a booby or two," he muttered as he fell into a deep but unsatisfying, albeit noisy, sleep, nestled in a downy pillow of great green stripes on an olive background, as cottony and billowy as a cloud aloft and alee.

He woke with a start when Nattering tiptoed in, tripping on his feet as usual as he turned toward his bed. "Was you asleep, brother" he asked maliciously, "or was that merely a hurricane-gale I heard passing through?" Sleep gone, Jack turned on the lamp and gazed at his friend. Stephen's grizzled wig was all ahoo, and his stockings, which Jack had clearly noticed to be inside-out earlier, were on rightwise, albeit befouled, ungartered, and downgyved to his ankles. Jack sniffed his friend suspiciously. "Molly Tarte, you cow-poxed son of a sea-farting dog!" he roared in sudden high humor.

Stephen grinned indignantly. "Thank you, my dear, for entertaining the admiral so long as you did," he murmured. "But it was strictly business, I do assure you. She has informed me of a capital assignment for us, which she learned of through her friend Miss Colebrook whose husband works for... for someone. You'll hear from the admiralty in the morning, I'm sure."

"For the love of God, tell me now," burst Jack. "I am with child to know what I'm to do next, for sure."

"I wouldn't doubt that for a moment," said Stephen sternly. "Twins, if anything. You certainly look to weigh seventeen stone and a pebble. But I am not at liberty to discuss the matter, as the details have not been ascertained yet. For now, get some rest, and perhaps tomorrow you will let me examine you concerning the impending child."

"For God's sake, Stephen, it's just an expression," Jack implored. But it was too late. Stephen had stopped his ears with balls of wax, and was oblivious to even Captain Audibly's sea-going bellow for information. Not for the first time that evening, Jack sighed, and then slipped easily into his customary sonorous slumber, goose fat dribbling pinguidly down his slack jowls. With the first nightly pang of dismay, Stephen heard Jack Audibly breathing, which breathing would soon take on flesh and bone and a phantasmagoric, horrific being of its own, while overhead outside, the gibbous moon shone luminescently as Orion aimed at his ever unseen prey across the nocturnal dome.

2

As the rosy-fingered dawn awoke, so did Captain Audibly, in a flush of good spirits. He was somewhat chagrined at not knowing what the future held, always regretting every semicolon in his career service, but high-spirited optimism was his natural state, and he grinned amiably at the sleeping form of Stephen Nattering. There was no use in waking the good doctor—it would put him in unpleasant fettle, from which no useful information could be dredged in any event, so the Captain ambled his huge frame to the breakfast room, humming snatches of Locatelli's long-lost A Major Quintet (*Trota*), where he consumed three fried eggs, accompanied by a pound of sausages and a large pitcher of orange juice, along with the usual muffins, cakelets, and breads, and a peanut butter and jelly sandwich (from which Quillick had trimmed the crusts for him precisely, in the nautical fashion). He absent-mindedly tapped the sandwich on the table, leaving a grape-coloured smear. "Damn," he swore. "I hate when that happens."

He began humming again as he waited for Quillick to clean the mess; Bach's The Art of the Fugue (*The Mandelbrot Set*) rumbled incongruously in his throat and filled the breakfast room, to the amusement of a group of officers trying to converse. When he was on his second pot of coffee and his first haunch of beef, Stephen shuffled in, wearing his scuffed slippers, scratching his stubble and yawning.

"Did you have a nice evening last night?" Jack inquired, hoping that this conversational gambit would put the doctor into a loquacious way.

"Quite nice, indeed, thankee," responded Stephen. "Are you asking out of concern for my enjoyment of the evening, or is this a mere conversational gambit designed to put me into a loquacious way?"

"Both," the captain replied honestly, unable to come up with a believable lie quickly enough.

"I don't know the details of the hypothetical voyage yet," Stephen said in anticipation of further questions. "You should be hearing from the Admiralty this morning." But then, knowing that this would not hold, he shifted his body and tipped the pot. "Faith, and did ye not leave me a droplet at all?"

Another pot of coffee was soon placed before them, and when both had sucked their mugs dry, and Stephen had polished off three kippered fishes (helped in the last by Audibly), Jack ventured to ask, "Do you know at all whereabouts we'll be going, or whatabouts we'll be about?"

"*Quo fas et gloria ducunt.* Something about the American colonies, to be sure," responded Stephen. "And as you know better than I, the dear *Aghast* (*fluctuat nec mergitur*) was bound for the knackers, to be chopped up for kindling. As she is of no further service to His Majesty, I believe she will be the vessel available for this particular mission."

"Oh, thank God, thank God for the dear barky *Aghast*," exclaimed Jack, his exuberance rising perceptibly. "I was feeling very hipped indeed about her fate, the dear old girl. I don't think I ever could bear to strike a match again, or use a toothpick, thinking it could be of the *Aghast*."

"Of course," Stephen went on, "when you see your documentation, you may choose not to participate. Sure and there's likely to be little glory or prize this time around, by the saints. You must not expect too much this time; it's not a glory mission."

"Do you mean don't eat my chickens before they've hatched, or is that the way it goes?" Jack inquired.

"Isn't it more like, don't count your chickens before they're eaten?" Stephen asked, smiling.

"Glory? Prize? Stephen!" exclaimed Jack indignantly. "D'ye really think that's what I'm about, after all these voyages we've been together on?"

"Not at all, my dear, not in the least. And yet, there's something to be said for a sweet prize, and a wee bit of glory never sat uncomfortable on anyone to my store of knowledge."

Mercedes-Benz came bouncing in, flushed with health and youthful lust, and gave both men generous hugs. "A letter!" she announced. "I breeng heem to you, yes capitano?" Glancing down, she shyly replaced her dusk-peachy bosom within her dress, tucking it below the necklace Captain Audibly had given her.

He gazed upon the necklace, and upon its surrounds, but only briefly. "By all means, bring him—I mean it, the letter—bring it to me as quickly as you please," he bellowed loudly at her.

She raced out, and returned bearing a crown and anchor-crested envelope.

"Excuse me, Doctor," he said, drinking the grease from the bottom of Nattering's plate of bacon, "I'll just be a few minutes." He walked quickly to the window on the other side of the breakfast room, and glancing around to ensure privacy, he studied the envelope. Gathering no meaningful information from the outside of the oblong white rectangle, he wiped bacon grease from his hands onto his trousers, preparatory to opening what was probably the most dear, precious document he would see in some time.

"Which I spent all night scrubbing my poor old fingers to the marrow on those trousers," grumbled Quillick from under that self-same table.

"Is that you, Quillick," roared Jack? "Come out from there and fetch me a napkin, if you please, and some toast and jam."

"Which I wuz just bringing as you said it, weren't I?" griped Quillick furiously.

"And then run along outside and stay there until you're sent for, d'ye hear me!" in an even louder, angrier voice than usual.

Pressured Quillick, the captain's steward, tried in vain to think of a reason to stay, any reason at all, any reasonable reason whatsoever, but nothing came into his head when he needed it most, so he left the breakfast room, grumbling loudly under and over his breath about the poor bleedin' lot of the poor bleedin' steward in His Majesty's poor bleedin' navy.

Captain Audibly once again devoted his attention to the envelope, going so far as to hold its sealed contents to his forehead, but again was totally unable to decipher its contents from the outside. Finally, he opened the envelope, removed the contents, and read:

By the Right Honorable Lord Camelford, Knight of the Bath, Admiral of the Red and Commander in Chief of His Majesty's Ships and Vessels employed and to be employed in the North Atlantic, etc., etc., etc.

Whereas Captain Jonathan Basil of His Majesty's Ship *Jimney* has deceased, and similarly has Commander Harry Featherstonhaugh of the *Windom* (32) ensuing from wounds suffered during the takings of *la Grenouille* and *La Baignoire,* and Jack Larmour with the brig Asgard having posted to the Mosquito Shore; and whereas *Whimsy* (64) being temporarily misplaced with Captain Finn Mac Cumaill aboard; and whereas Mr. Pulliam has lost the *Survey* (48) to the enemy in *l'Usurpateur;* and whereas Captains Yardley and Smithson have their paperwork in the civil service, probably never to be extricated in time to be of any civil service; and whereas there being no other rated Captains available within many distant leagues of the home waters;

You are hereby required and directed to proceed on board the *Aghast* and take upon you the Charge and Command of Captain of her; willing and requiring all the Officers and Company belonging to said *Aghast* to behave themselves in their several Employments with all due Respect and Obedience to you their Captain; and you likewise to observe as well the General Printed Instructions as what Orders and Directions you may from time to time receive from any your superior Officer for His Majesty's Service. Your mission will be to ply off the waters of the New World colonies, and from Maryland to Florida in particular, harassing their shipping and installations, blockading their mercantile ports, and impressing whatever men you choose to consider British for His Majesty's

Navy. You will carry with you the physician Nattering, and will accommodate his particular needs as His Majesty's representative. You will receive further, more specific instructions Orally. Hereof nor you nor any of you may fail as you will answer the contrary at your Peril.

And for so doing this shall be your Order.

Given on board the *Destination* at sea, 14th February, 1814.

To Jack Audibly, Esqr, hereby appointed Captain of His Majesty's Ship *Aghast*

By command of Richard Patrick Russ, First Lord of the Admiralty.

There followed a section on secret signals that was indecipherable, until Jack cleverly turned the sheet aloft and alow. The secret part of the document had been cleverly written upside down, da Vinci style, to prevent its being known if the document had fallen into enemy hands; (the French never had been known to scruple at opening another's private mail). It read, in part:

Upon the encounter of two ships, not immediately recognizing one from the other: the first ship to see the other shall hoist a green and orange flag from the topmost royal mast, and shall allow the mast to fall to the deck. To be <u>answered</u>, if a friendly ship, by the tossing overboard of the youngest member of the ship's boys. The first ship, if friend, shall despatch a gig to fetch the boy to safety, if convenient. If not, the ship's men shall sing *The Battle of the Nile*[1], reprinted below, as signal to the second ship to rescue its own

---

[1] *THE BATTLE OF THE NILE*

Twas on the ninth day of August in the year ninety-eight
We'll sing the praise of Nelson and the bold British fleet;
For the victory we've gained o'er the rebellious crew,
And to the Mediterranean Sea, brave boys, we'll bid adieu.

chorus: So come, you British tars, let your hands and hearts agree
To protect the lives and liberties of the mother country.

younker, should they so desire. As further evidence of friendly status, the crew of the second ship shall join in the singing, and all hands shall get rousingly drunk.

Jack Audibly reread the letter. He reread it again, and yet again. He followed the text with his finger, and mouthed the words subvocally. A huge joy surged within his breast. His passion for music rose within him, swelling his already massive upper thighs. He roared with laughter, and when Mercedes-Benz came running to see what the hullabaloo was about, he hugged her with all his strength.

At four o'clock that evening he brought that fleet in sight
And like undaunted heroes we were eager for the fight,
They were lying at an anchor near the Egyptian shore,
Superior to the British fleet, and to take us they made sure.

Our noble captain he was slain soon after we began;
Brave Cuthbert in succession he boldly took command,
For four full hours that evening we engaged them on the main,
And early the next morning we renewed the fight again.

Full fifty seamen we had slain, which grieved our hearts full sore
Two hundred more were wounded, lay bleeding in their gore.
But early the next morning most glorious to see
Our British ships of war, brave boys, were crowned with victory.

Buonaparte's pride we demolished, and that very soon
We made his crew to rue the day that they ever left Toulon,
But now he's got among the Turks where he'll be forced to stay
And besides he has lost the title of The Conqueror of Italy.

A building castles in the air and doing these great feats,
And threatening of Albania's plans in our united states,
Planting the Tree of Liberty all on our native shore,
But Nelson's stars have nipped the bud will never flourish more.

And now the fight is over and we have gained the day
Nine sails we took and four we burnt, the rest they ran away.
But when we come home to England, so loudly we will sing,
"Success to our Majestic, boys, and long live George the King!"

"Stephen," he roared, after reviving Mercedes-Benz. "Make haste, make extraordinary haste. There's not a moment to be lost! We must run like your stockings!"

"But my dear," sputtered Stephen, glancing down and tucking his legs under him. "There's quite some time to be lost. Sure, and don't eat the horse before the cart," he said, hunching his shoulders protectively over the remains of his breakfast. "We can't leave until I speak with my contact person at London next week, for the details of my part of the assignment." He poured himself another mug of coffee, and quickly snatched at his remaining chicken leg as Audibly returned toward the table with visible lust in his eye. "We have time sure to finish our breakfast, and then we can take a chaise or a barouche to Cedargrove Cottage, and see our dear wives before ever we can leave. And I have a mosquito for Blaine and I can't possibly leave England before I deliver it into his hands. Now don't pout at me for the delay. Sure, and it's uneasy lies the head that wears a frown."

Doctor Nattering also had a sealed letter. Fortunately for Mercedes-Benz, who was gasping and examining her ribs, he received it with taciturn gratitude, and retreated to the reading room to examine it. It was short —details to be provided later—and in code. The message read:

"O-gay oo-tay merica-yay and-way ork-way ith-way e-thay eek-cray indians-way." He sighed sadly, wiped his hands on his coat, knuckled his temples, and opened his code book to the Catalonian Jeringoza deciphering section.

Jack Audibly's heart, lungs, and essence were filled with ebullience and joy, and he sang aloud as he scraped crumbs from the table and floor, already planning his course across the Atlantic. He was hellfire to begin the voyage; a rolling ship gathers no doldrum-weed; it was just like Stephen to delay him interminably. Nattering was as slow as the offspring of a British Admiralty civil servant and a French lady of leisure. An inchoate jest rose in his mind, and he chuckled prematurely, dispelling the conclusion. Try as he might, he couldn't recapture the brilliance of his flash, but he laughed heartily for it anyhow. Something about Stephen moving at the speed of darkness, but he couldn't quite cross the t on it. He rubbed his fingers on a few of Stephen's rosin-bags in his pockets, gazing furtively about lest Stephen should appear to reclaim the bags, and strode out happily.

The wind picked up some cloud contrails and blew them across the scuddering sky, but Jack Audibly's heart flew faster than ever the contrails could navigate the celest as he returned to his room at the Clown for a matitudinal snack.

3

Captain Audibly was of a naturally cheerful nature, never one to dwell on difficulties longer than it took to resolve them, and ever seizing on opportunities for joy, passionate good will, even ecstasy over what would be trifles to others. It was well-known by those who loved him that he derived a greater pleasure from a smaller stream of wit than geese or hyenas or even women did.

The promised use of the *Aghast* was a sheer joy to him. He loved the *Aghast* as other men loved a good cigar or a fertile woman or a decent hunting dog; and it had pained him to his soul to have her sold out of the service and treated unkindly. He would, of course, have accepted any assignment with any promise of service to homeland, continued employment, along with the possibility of bloodshed, prize (the Royal Navy's version of trick-or-treating on the high seas), glory, terrorism, floggings, keelhaulings, and conquest. This, however, was the sweetest assignment he could covet. He had earlier been considering a letter to the Admiralty along the lines of the one Nelson had reportedly written:

"If your Lordships should be pleased to appoint me to a cockle-boat I shall feel grateful."[2]

"That's putting it a bit strong," Jack reflected. "I should not be grateful for a cockle-boat, but perhaps he was being metaphysical . . . or is it metabolical? Anyway, the one having to do with a figure of speech, of saying one thing and meaning another... or is that flying under false colors, to say one thing... " Reflecting was difficult on a practically empty stomach.

But the *Aghast*! The dear, sweet *Aghast*! He had not expected so sweet a ship. And the West Atlantic! What absolute joy to be

---

[2] Captain Horatio Nelson to the Board of Admiralty, from Burnham Thorpe, Norfolk, 5th December, 1792. Pocock, Tom, *Horatio Nelson*, Alfred A. Knopf, New York, 1988, p. 76.

used in the West Atlantic, where the war was not going well, and a man of his talents could be of faithful service to England! He knew for certain that the Crown was earth's last, best hope for peace. The joyous music of Locatelli's soon-to-be-lost tone poem *Also Sprach Buonaparte* echoed through his brain as he exulted in his commission.

But before long, Captain Audibly's natural exuberance had begun to pall, along with his constitution. How on earth was he to find a complement of some two hundred men and officers, some of whom could actually hand, reef and steer, in what remained of England's male population was beyond him. The sun had not set on the Empire, but it was certainly dim over Captain Audibly's head as he turned the problem over in his mutton-stuffed mind. He decided to take a turn along the quay; sea air always had a restorative effect on his constitution.

The crisp winter air felt like refreshing wine on his cheeks as he left the overheated inn with a feeling of satisfaction. The winter sky was a huge porcelain blue bowl overhead; pale, almost luminous to the sides, no doubt reflecting the rare snow that had fallen during the night, which was already gone from the city.

Far, far up in the middle of that dome, safely beyond incidental musket range, a flight of seven wild geese, two to one side of the vee leader and four to the other, made its way across from one inlet to another.

Audibly felt a touch of vertigo, as if he were falling into that porcelain bowl, and reflected that he had not yet regained his land legs, quite forgetting the bottle of white, the two of burgundy, and the cognac he had used to moisten the path of his mid-morning snack of oysters, clams, and a small but satisfying cow.

A bright swirl of white against the blue of sky and sea —a dozen seagulls wheeled at the rear of the inn Jack had just vacated. The tide was low, exposing the midden of shells where he had been tossing, over his shoulder, the remnants from his repast.

Today, however, the sea air did little for his mood. Instantly he stepped outside, he began attracting a swarm. Bees and wasps were always attracted to Jack Audibly; he brushed them away impatiently, thereby angering them to greater heights of aggression. Jack walked along the quay, small animals fleeing in his wake. The quay was full of men, but they were not for him. Men by the dozens, by the scores, but they were either unsuitable or they belonged to another ship, to another captain. He looked hungrily at them, devoured them with his eyes the way a harlot might, even drooled over some, but not even a one did he espy that he could recruit to his purposes. The sun shone hotly, and hotly did Captain Audibly eye the men he saw, but he did not see a solution to the problem. He had a ship to man, but no men to man her. A flaxen-haired, large-boned buxom woman looked askance at him, smiling. By her side, a small fluffy dog capered and pranced, as if defying the world to boot him into the sea. His eye gleamed as he examined her, but regulations prohibited his pressing her.

"Am I to go to sea for six months with a bleeding press-crew?" he agonized. If requested, the press-gang would seize for him seamen, or any watermen, otherwise employed or not, who could not produce certificates of exemption. But they would be unwilling to serve, resentful, hard in spirit, downcast, unsuited for the sort of voyage he best enjoyed. Press-gangs were most prone to raid taverns and brothels, taking the lowest form of man England had to offer. Worse: if driven to such desperate measures, he would be forced to accept convicts sent by the magistrates for service in the Navy in lieu of prison—supposedly only minor miscreants and malfeasants would be given him, but he had known highwaymen, cut-throats, slime-scumbags of the worst magnitude, brutal murderers, even barristers and schoolteachers to be foisted onto the unwilling sea-captains of his experience when the magistrates chose to empty their gaols of empty-bellied, low-life, useless swine who would eat the prison's bread without expectation of service in return. Land-lubbers! Useless, woebegotten, dribbling, grass-combing, vomitous land-lubbers! It would not do at all. He had to find sailors before he could sail. But how in God's name, under the sheer blue sky, was he to succeed in doing so?

As he mulled the matter, a group of young men turned the corner and entered the road he was on. "Press those men, Mr. Blonden!" he roared to his coxswain.

"Press me, thir," lisped the closest of the men. "Press me hard, if you pleathe. Nothing would please us more than six months in a small ship with two hundred musty, sweaty men."

Audibly and Blonden both ran, the young men in close pursuit. They lost their pursuers, eventually, and immediately spotted a muscular young man, about twenty years of age, meandering along the quay. Audibly approached him, and inquired politely as to his availability for service in the Royal Navy.

"I'd like to oblige, matey," responded that worthy, "but I promised me mum I'd stay at home and attend to my chores until I reach thirty."

"Oh," said Audibly, disappointed. He brightened, however, upon spotting another likely young candidate.

"So sorry, sport," said the young man. "I'd enjoy a tour in the Navy, truly I would, but my wife is expecting a baby, and I'd like to be close at hand, to help her with changing the nappies, walk the baby when he's colicky, burp him when he's spitty, and so on."

"I'd be glad to serve," responded yet another would-be hero. "Have to tell you, though, that I'm an ethical ovo-lacto-vegetarian—I think eating the flesh of once-living creatures is cruel and unacceptable. D'ye suppose your cook could keep me in a sustainable diet of veggies and beans and nuts and seeds and whole-grained breads?"

Another likely candidate was rejected when Captain Audibly detected a whiff of alcohol on the man's breath; yet another because his shoes were unshined; and yet another because, after a lengthy but fruitless interview, Audibly determined that the young seaman's political views were quite antithetical to his own. Finding suitable manpower to crew a sea voyage was getting quite difficult indeed.

The next man they attempted to press bowed down repeatedly to them, murmuring "Krishna Krishna Hare Krishna," and unfortunately, tore a hole in Captain Audibly's coat while fastening a flower into his lapel and stuffing his pockets with leaflets.

Audibly did not wish to offend the man, but declined to make a cash offering; fortunately, however, the young man blessed their upcoming voyage anyway.

Audibly and Blonden did find one appropriately hirsute candidate eventually, and were escorting him to the dock, but he tripped and fell, and broke a fingernail, so they released him to return home and file it down, and the scoundrel never returned.

The last thing Jack Audibly saw as they left the quay was the buxom woman's dog, no longer capering, no longer fluffy, crawling bedraggled from the sea, while a stolid marine watched, waiting to boot him back in.

As expected, Stephen Nattering was of no use whatsoever. "Never fear, my sweet," said Stephen. "The men always seem to appear on the ships, by my word. I don't know where they come from, but every time I've come on board a ship, it has had a complement of sailors."

Jack stared at him, aghast. "D'ye think they just appear, upon my word? Are you gaming with me?"

One look at Stephen, however, assured him that this remark, like so many others he had made during their long, enduring friendship, was entirely guileless. "I'll tell you a secret," Jack confided. "There's a reason there are men on a ship, just as there's a reason there are spars, masts, cordage, shells, cannons, salt beef, dried peas and biscuit on a ship. Would you care for me to tell you the secret?"

"I should like it of all things. Prithee, explain."

"The men are on the ship because the captain got them on the ship. The stores are on the ship because someone got them, someone ordered them put on the ship, someone put them on the ship. They do not, for all love, just appear."

"Oh," said Stephen.

"And neither more than these commodities do human commodities just appear. They have to be gotten, do you see, gotten by a Captain who wants to man his ship. And at this time, there are no men to be gotten. They can't be gotten if they aren't there, d'ye follow?"

"I believe I do," said Stephen, huffily at being condescended to. "I believe I do follow indeed. But I am confident that when we are in Hampshire, or perchance in Portsmouth, perhaps some young fellows may show up, faith. There's still plenty of time, you know."

Jack was not soothed by this. Stephen, seeing the troubled look on Jack's usually genial countenance, tried to help as best he could. "What do you suppose Lord Nelson, that great man, would have done in such a situation? Sure, if you could put yourself in his mind you could find solutions a-plenty to all your nautical conundrums."

"It surprises me that you even know of Nelson," Jack ventured.

"Of course I know of Nelson," Stephen brindled. "He's the chap who set to sea with Eugene Poole, the great naturalist of the world, and as I recall, Nelson did rush the poor man out of Copenhagen before ever he had time to complete cataloguing the earthworms of that great city."

"I met Nelson once, you know," said Jack, eagerly, his eyes glowing. "Did I ever mention it before?"

"Not above two hundred times, I'm sure," replied Stephen. "But I forgot the details. Shall you recount the meeting for me? I should certainly enjoy the hearing of it, of all things."

"He spoke to me just briefly, of course. He was busy dining with others, but I remember every syllable with reverence."

"What was it he said to you?" asked Stephen. "Would it in any way bear on the current problem of staffing a ship? He is said to be an excellent strategist and thinker, as you no doubt already know. I've heard, in fact, that he knew the answer to that famous Zen paradox, you know the one, and that he was able to apply that sort of thinking to modern naval challenges."

"He looked directly at me, and said 'You goddam fat clumsy lobscouse—you've quite spilt the salt.' But he said it in so kindly a manner that I shall never forget his goodness."

Stephen pondered. "It don't rightly bear on the manpower question, does it?" He scratched his head. A louse crawled down, and he snatched at it fondly. *"Pediculus humanus capitis,"* he murmured fondly. "In no way to be confused with *Pediculus humanus corporis*, at all. Of the order Anoplura, of course. I'll save it for Banks. He'll be so glad to have it." He referred, of course, to Joseph Banks, the naturalist who had accompanied Cook to Australia, and was a fellow member of the Royal Society. He examined the louse carefully. It appeared to have no gross deformities, blemishes, scars, or other distinguishing features. All six of its legs were there, intact, the eyes were unclouded, unoccluded, and its gorge of human blood rendered it slow, but not at all turgid. He wrapped it carefully in his handkerchief, and tucked it into his pocket. "Don't worry your head about sailors. I'm sure they'll turn up, as they always have done so. And you don't want to be fixating yourself on the numbers of men, neither. Remember, too many cooks spoil the broth."

Jack Audibly had little faith in Stephen's expectations of matters naval, and didn't credit the aphorism. He had no notion of the existence of too many cooks, nor too many sailors; nor did he think that the addition of cooks would spoil a brothel—if anything could improve a brothel, it would be cooks. But there was nothing for it anyway, so they quickly prepared to return home for fond farewells to their beloved wives. The sky overhead was no less blue than usual, the breezes blew in their customary fashion for the time of year, the clouds assumed their regular formations in response to meteorological considerations; but Jack Audibly was too preoccupied with the question of manpower to notice, care, comment, or enjoy. He should have delighted in the coming reunion with dear Sophie, but his heart was heavy with the burdens of impending command. If, that is, he could find minds and souls, but especially bodies, warm, breathing, preferably sturdy, muscular, able seaman English male bodies, to command. He looked up to the floating cirrus clouds, flying across the sky like circus trapeze artists. The floating cirrus clouds looked back down on him, but did not answer his unspoken plaint.

4

As some of the mist began to lift, weak sunlight came into the chill morning. Clump by ragged clump of untrimmed grass it picked out, giving each blade on one side a distinct silver gleam. Clumps of cedar branch were black in their own shadow. On the edge of the fog, the paler-needled pines were nearly invisible. Deeper into the mists, the great oaks of the region could not be seen, only their ancient voices heard, in a loud, continuing drip-drip.

Insouciant, a sparrow trotted up the rutted roadway between the puddles, seemingly immune to touch of either mist or mud. For once, he moved in his quick hop, without a sound.

As quick and alert as Jack Audibly was, he could not catch Stephen Nattering who, upon boarding the chaise for the ride to Cedargrove Cottage in Hampshire, caught his heel on the step and plunged headlong against the side of the door. Jack snatched at him, but the damage had been done - blood and sanies poured crimson from Stephen's forehead, and he was quite dazed as Jack arighted him with a jerk of his massive forearm.

"I didn't notice that the step was so high," muttered Stephen, pressing his filthy handkerchief to his forehead. Jack watched, in horrified anguish, as Stephen's collection of moths, maggots, clumps of sloth-fur, a newt's preserved eye, the toe of a frog, a bat's two wings as well as his wool, an unidentifiable tongue, lice and Norwegian cockroaches crawled down or fell from their place of confinement in the handkerchief when it was unfurled. He considered recapturing the various species as a service to his dear friend and the friends of his friend, but was frozen in place at the sight of a scorpion crawling from the crease, its stinger poised high in its slow, dignified exit. He next thought to at least replace the already blood-soaked cloth with his own black-and-white Nelson-checkered neckcloth, but out of deference to Quillick, his steward, he stayed his hand.

"Did you fall?" Jack inquired.

"I suppose I may have," responded Stephen. "I didn't quite observe. Did I?"

"Are you all right?" Jack asked, not a little anxiously. With the acute manpower shortages already facing him, he hoped earnestly not to require also to replace his ship's doctor, his dearest friend and companion. Friends could come and go, but a ship's surgeon whose only vice was mainstreaming narcotic addiction would be a sore loss. Stephen, in fact, was more than a surgeon—he was a physician, certified, and when not in the depths of Nepenthe, was very highly valued by the men.

"Upon my word, never better, never better," answered Stephen with obviously false cheerfulness. And in fact, despite the scarlet gush and gouts of lymph and flesh pouring forth, his wound seemed less deep than many Jack had seen Stephen to inflict upon himself when entering or exiting a vehicle, landborn or seagoing, moving or stationery. Indeed, Stephen had tripped and fallen in trabacaloes in the Adriatic, tartans in the Gulf of Lions, terranovas off the banks of Newfoundland, xebecs and settees along the whole of the Spanish coast, bucentaurs in Venice, funneys in Cambridge, jangadas off Portugal, as well as dozens, hordes of feluccas, pinks, polacres, polacre-settees, houarios, bean-cods, cats, herring-busses, long-boats, launches, revenue cutters, yawls, gigs, canoes, jolly-boats, doggers, schuyts, howkers, bugalets, barquentines, carrakes, barges and balyngers, dromonds, gaboards, and bomb-ketches for as long as Jack had known him, fell down at the mere mention of a sea-going vessel, and with God's blessing, would ever continue to do so, Jack thought fondly. Unhappily, a loving Irish nanny had long ago blessed young Stephen with the benediction "May the road rise up to meet you," and thereafter not only roads, but seas, puddles, mudwallows, thank-you-ma'ams, minor surface variegations, assorted animals, and even breezes and wisps had been rising up to meet him ever since.

"A mere flesh-cut," Stephen soothed. "If ye'll be kind enough to hold my looking glass up for me, I'll just insert a round few stitches in meself and be none the worse for wear." He absently wiped the point of his needle off on his trousers, and proceeded to thread it. "Is this sharp enough, d'ye think?" he asked, jabbing Jack hard with the needle.

"Yipe, ye blamed _____ whey-faced whoreson!" Jack yowled. "For all the times you've done that, I never quite come to expect it. Yes, it's sharp enough, I suppose. You know I'm not an expert on medical matters, but I suppose it's sharp enough to penetrate even your damned scaly old flesh. Ye've sewn me up with considerably duller, you know."

Stephen chuckled, and began sewing his forehead together, holding the lips of the wound with one hand and stitching with the other. "Mind, <u>avast</u>, as we say in the navy, avast ye jogging the glass so. Just hold it steady, for the love of the saints." He stitched quickly at first, but a glance at Jack Audibly's formerly ruddy face, now a ghastly yellow, bug-eyed, bilious, vertitiginous visage, quite slowed his work.

"How many more stitches," Jack asked wanly.

"Not above a dozen," Stephen mumbled. Chuckling to himself evilly, he jabbed at himself and cried out, winced, flinched... carefully bringing his good friend right to the very precipice of swooning before at great length finishing the process. "Would you mind tying me off with a sound nautical granny knot?" he asked with over-feigned innocence. "The Dear One knows I've learned all sorts of beautiful, mariner-type navy knots by now, during the course of my many sea-voyages, but you do it so much prettier, neater and better..."

"Jack! If you please—lean out leeward of the carriage to do that!"

"Are ye feeling a wee bit better now," Stephen asked?

Jack did not answer, but mechanically tied seven loops of hemp around each of Stephen's wrists and ankles, to prevent him falling out of the chaise at every bump and turn, tying them off to the corners of the chaise. The driver came around to see what the ruckus was about, stared for several long moments at Jack's ashen face, at Stephen, bound and bleeding eloquently and steadily despite his sutures and ministrations, and then retreated to his box, mumbling about all the assorted goddammed buggery perverts he had had to put up with in his chaise, but this did beat all, did beat all, never saw the like...

The journey proceeded as uneventfully as could be hoped for. Captain Audibly snored with even greater than usual intensity, volume, sonorousness, and mournful plangency, happily dreaming of going to America and eating Babe, the blue ox, working his jaws and salivating as he slept; Stephen Nattering, unable to stop his ears with wax as was his custom when sharing a chaise with the Captain, being bound by the wrists, longed for his customary pint of laudanum, the tincture of opium which served so well in such circumstances in granting him a drop of sleep. Although Captain Audibly oft-times disapproved of his physician's personal use of opium, Stephen stoutly maintained that it was a harmless vice, far preferable to the more common habit in the Royal Navy of smoking or sucking on pricks. He thought longingly of noble Homer's seamen, their master lashed to the mast, but at least having had their ears blessedly filled with sweet, cloying wax; longingly, longingly, long into the long night. "Circe's song may have turned men into swine," he mused, "But dear Jack's song will soon turn me deaf as a post-captain." He thought the matter through. "That's not the way it goes, sure, but it certainly serves."

As the minutes stretched into hours, and interminable hours at that, his mind turned over images of the blind poet, thence to the one-eyed giant he wrote about, thence to Jack's hero, Admiral Nelson, but try as he might, he could not turn the metaphor into a phrase worth repeating in the morning.

With the stamp and clash of Jack's nocturnal song trumpeting in his ears from a distance of one-quarter of a meter ("but with no sense of meter at all, no more than when first we met"), Stephen slowly endured the night. He wondered that birds did not plummet from the sky, struck dead by the shock waves as Jack Audibly snored below them. Hearing Jack snore was like hearing the very earth sundered—the Himalayas splitting the floor of the sea and shouldering their massive way remorselessly into the aching heights; the glaciers calving from the walls of Antarctica were a gentle whisper in comparison.

At great length, the black and white checquered walls of Cedargrove Cottage hove themselves into view on the horizon, barely visible through the sudden drenching downpour that had come on in the night, gusting, pelting rain that ran off the road before them in great torrential rivulets; but unmistakably it was Cedargrove Cottage, at last.

And what a sight they did behold! Jack, coming awake, looked at Stephen to see if he was still in the chaise or had fallen out despite the lashing; relieved, he glanced out at the cottage through the downpour, and nearly fell out of the chaise himself!

"What in tarnation? What the blooming bleeding tarnation," Jack quivered at the most unusual sight he'd ever clapped his eyes upon. Even Stephen, experienced to all the strangest sights that nineteen sea-going voyages to all parts of the world could reveal to him, was mesmerized, and unaccustomedly silent at the spectacle that greeted them through the pluvial deluge of the morn, in plumbaginous wet mantle clad.

5

How could Captain Audibly fail to take ecstatic joy at the sight he beheld that rainy, gloomy, damp morning, stepping down from the carriage with Stephen Nattering slung over his back like a sack of wet sailcloth? Who in a right turn of mind could scruple to delight at the long-awaited sight of his wife—his precious, dear, adored, sweet wife—and his children: fat, good-natured, moon-faced Georges, aged seven, and the eight-year-old turnip-nosed twin girls, Carlotta and Fancy, the females, the swabs; and after all his exhausting hours and days of worrying about manpower, how could it not soar his heart and spirits to see the glorious sight of *Aghasts*: glorious, muscular, manly, virile, sweaty, fuggy; his hand-picked crew—able seamen one and all—<u>competent</u>, happy, sweet *Aghasts*! As far as his eye could see—they must all two hundred be there, lying about on the wet grass, gammoning, dancing; but unhappily, most of them coming the fool, cavorting around poor, dear, soggy Sophie, standing out in the rain, all vying with each other to shield her head from the rain with torn pieces of tarpaulin and sailcloth. Fancy and Carlotta were both stamping in puddles in the downpour in their stockinged feet, trying to catch the rainwater in their mouths and laughing like gibbons; while Georges was struggling to eat a rain-soaked potpie; soggy as it was, he was accustomed to English fare and sog didn't seem to signify.

"Silence fore and aft," Jack boomed. "What the h___ is going on here?" He began cursing at full throttle, that curiously blue sailor's string of profanity that had graced the decks of naval vessels from the first syllable of recorded mariner history. At the onslaught, several girls jumped up from under the *Aghasts*, startled at the sight of so much gold braid on clean blue sleeve, and ran off, tugging at their clothes and giggling. Jack continued to curse, growing louder, more vehement, and considerably more colorful in his similes and metaphors. Sophie tried in vain to cover the girls' ears, but since the *Aghast* sailors had already been in town for more than twenty- four hours, the girls had already acquired a vocabulary of profanity that far exceeded anything Jack Audibly had ever heard or said in his twenty-odd years in the British Royal Navy.

Eventually, the hullabaloo settled down, the fools quietened, the gamboling and womanizing ceased, and the story came to light of day. When the *Aghast* had been condemned out of the service, and no other ship had been available to Captain Audibly's command, the crew been impressed into the *Sailnought* (42), Captain Suckling; had sailed not two days before being captured off Ushant ("Ile D'ouessant," Jack hissed in response to Stephen's quizzical eyebrow) by the French in the *Merde* (42), and had been imprisoned. Fortunately, Diana Villiers-Todd-Burton-Canning-Johnstone-Johnson-Onassis-Nattering heard of this, and, knowing how much her incumbent husband loved these men, had purchased them out of captivity, pawning her huge diamond necklace, the Blue Willie[3], to do so, having previously dissolved in brandy and consumed all her pearls. So the *Aghast*-men came back to Cedargrove Cottage, where Diana lived with her cousin Sophie, Jack's wife, and hoping there to do the dear ladies a service out of gratitude, as well as duty to their captain. It hit upon them that since the roof leaked something fierce, they might be able to repair it. They had struck the roof down only yesterday, in fair shining innublious weather, preparatory to fixing it, when disaster struck, in the appearance of Captain Picard. Picard was manning up his vessel *Enterprise*, 61, and although he had an amazingly full complement of men, he did not scruple to impress straightaway Mr. Mason, the *Aghast*'s carpenter; his own carpenter, Woodenhead Belubberly, having been laid alow by the severest case of shingles his doctor had ever seen. The scrub Picard—carpenters were supposed to be warranted to their ships, as standing officers, although that usually did not stand in the way of lowlife scum such

---

[3]   So named after the effect of mercuric chloride, Dr. Nattering's standard treatment for syphilis, on the sailor's affected organ.

as bald-headed Picard—"what a pair of brass four-pounders HE must have amidships," Jack muttered to himself. Thus, the roof was down, the rain had been pouring in all night and day, and none among them had the skills to repair it without the carpenter and his tools, although they had efforted mightily with knotted ropes, hemp, and cordage, and bits of canvas, which could be seen from the ground level to be flapping soddenly from the beams.

Meanwhile, the girls, in their excitement over seeing their father once again, after an absence of several months, had begun their usual quarreling, their childish vocabularies enhanced by the presence of the *Aghasts* for the past four and twenty hours.

"Mama," screeched Carlotta, her wet hair streaming down her chubby cheeks, "That goddammed bosun's hemorrhoid Fancy has took my goddammed toy boat!"

"Not so, Mama," cried Fancy piteously, her own sodden tresses caught up in her nose mucous. "Carlotta's the syphilitic whore of the world who pulled my hair."

"Thou," said Carlotta calmly, pointing her finger to her twin sister, "Art the offspring of an indigent vole and a desperate cat."

"Thou," said Fancy, smiling in the spirit of the game, "art the offspring of a debauched sloth and an ersatz brown bear."

Georges, having finished his potpie, also had a piece to add. Tugging at Sophie's wet dress, bawling loudly, he sobbed "Mama, Fancy called me an ox-pus whoreson. What's a whoreson, Mama?"

Sophie, vexed beyond words, just stared in horrified disbelief at her children. Horrified the more so, if such was possible, as she became painfully aware of the prying eyes and ears of her mother, the dowager Williams (to whom some of these epithets might more rightfully apply), who was taking it all in with the rapt attention of one pretending to have never heard such language in her own long-vanished day, and the vicar, who had dropped by to say "how-do" having seen the chaise arrive that morning.

"Go ask your father," she finally choked out.

"Come here, son," said Jack kindly. "Run along to the barn as quick as you please and fetch me the axe and some ha'penny nails. We'll have the roof rigged shipshape and tidy before you can say . . . " But in his sore vexation at the spectacle, he was unable to think of a suitable word of the proper length and appropriate for his children's ears.

"Not in your best scraper, you ain't!" muttered Quillick, but he lost his moral advantage when he slipped in the wet grass and fell arsy-versy, accompanied by the children merrily trilling, almost in unison, "Surely you must blush for your fall," and Stephen's saturnine advice, "You must keep one hand for the land and the other for yourself."

Jack went into the cottage to surveil the damage. It was even worse than he had expected from outside, far worse. The rainwater poured in throughout the length and breadth of the cottage. All the furniture, all their belongings, all their accommodations were soaked through and through. The four-poster where he had bedded Sophie on their wedding night was awash, and the delicate white curtains he had embroidered so painstakingly when they settled at Cedargrove were ruined. Chairs, tables, and cabinets were floating down rivers in the hallways, bumping incongruously against the walls along the way; Fancy's Christening gown washed underfoot, and he snatched at Georges' little silver cup as it swept by in a torrent. He watched with interest as some jars of peach preserve floated by, and with even more interest as some fatty pork sausages trailed after, looping around the edges of the furniture and flinging free. He saw the bolt of silk fabric he had bought for Clarissa Oakes - he had given Sophie the remnants, and away they floated; Sophie's dresses, shifts, nightclothes, and unmentionables had washed out of the closets, and had clogged into a corner of her chamber, and bits of wood and stone and wall and floor were coursing throughout the house, if what remained could indeed still be termed a house. The servants, Deukalion and his wife Pyrrha, were of little help, snatching ineffectually at random items that streamed past.

Outside, the *Aghasts* had abruptly sobered themselves, standing overly erect as men do when conscious of a buzzing in their heads from overindulgence in the grapes of their Captain's wrath. They had drawn themselves up in mustered divisions, each toeing an imaginary line in the wet grass, and awaited orders. Jack stood at the highest point remaining in the house, and began issuing instructions in a steady stream, interspersed with comments about the probable species of parentage of each man named. Stephen watched with interest, providing the Latin terminology for each genus and species named in a curiously monotonous undertone, as if providing information of urgent need to the gentlemen named. Fancy and Carlotta, each riding comfortably now on one of Jack Audibly's broad shoulders, gaped and gawked at the spectacle of two hundred men acting now as with a single mind, as they hewed, hammered, nailed, and in amazingly rapid procession, raised a roof over the remains of Cedargrove Cottage. Georges, meanwhile, ran about self-importantly behind the men's heels, gleefully repeating the Captain's orders, as relayed in succession by lieutenants and officers and midshipmen, in his most piping nasal falsetto.

Post nubila Phoebus —As the last nail was hammered home, it was accompanied by a final, horrendous clap of thunder, and then the rain stopped, and the sun beamed forth in its accustomed place. Water swept out of the cottage in coursing rivulets under the mops and brooms and swabs of the manly men of His Majesty's Ship *Aghast*, and all present were aware of the finally happy, exuberantly happy face of Captain Jack Audibly, RN, who beamed and laughed aloud in the sheer, unmitigated delight of seeing wife, son, daughters, home and hearth, and a full crew of able seamen in all their splendiferous soddenness, God bless them every one!

6

It was glorious to be home, tubbed, scrubbed and rubbed by the gentle loving hands of his wife, viewing with satisfaction the growth of his children since last he had clapped eyes on them; Lord how they had grown in four months! Sophie had finally cut Georges' golden curls, and looking upon him fondly, Jack could foresee the manly chap he would someday grow into—already his feet had grown two sizes in four months, and he would soon grow into those feet. Jack shivered with the qualm of his children growing to adulthood in his absence; but duty called, repeatedly, and it was hard enough to hold his own place on the advancement list with the fullest service he could beg, cajole, wheedle from the Admiralty Board. He roughhoused with the children, rolling on the floor, pinning Georges effortlessly (for now!) while the girls straddled his stomach, trying to tickle him without being tickled in turn. He tried the children on their lessons; Fancy and Carlotta had already mastered their alphabets and a few words of French, while Georges was abysmally lost at ciphers and numbers, looked blank at the mention of Kings before his namesake the Third, but could recount with heart-gladdening gusto Nelson's great Battle of the Nile (in which Jack had served as lieutenant in the *Leander* (50)), the Battle of Copenhagen, and of course, Trafalgar; naming all the ships and their varying positions throughout the battles with remarkable accuracy. He could locate most named sites on the map on the library wall, and seemed right smart at whatever he actually turned his mind to. He had carved a boat from the trunk of a small oak tree, and had done a creditable job in masting and sheeting her, and could already (at seven!) sail her around the small lake in fair breezes. All three could read pieces from the holy Bible, and quote their favorite lines. Jack swelled with pride and joy at the sight of his children; he wished he could stay longer with them, and with dear, dear Sophie, of course. He still had trouble telling the girls apart, but most of the time he got Georges right, although he took him for Fancy once, when Georges wore a shirt of blue. He gave them a holiday from their lessons until his departure date, so they could spend time with him and his men, learning first-hand the ways of the sailor. The men had been adjured to clean, gentlemanly language at Sophie's request, and although they forgot themselves more than once in each utterance, they were clearly trying their best, and hardly ever failed to say "Excuse, ma'am" when their slips were pointed out to them by subtle shudders, gasps, or blank, baffled expressions.

Baretta Blondin took the opportunity to give Georges some boxing lessons, and Jack was gratified to see the boy step up manfully, and go at it. His limbs were already lengthening, his muscles starting to cord, and he was not afraid to absorb a few gentle blows in order to deliver a few of his own in turn. "All he needs is a few more years of growth, some training, and a bit of experience, and he'll not be the runt of the midshipman's berth, even at twelve," Jack considered. "But his schooling will have to be stepped up a fair pace. I'll be goddammed if I'll send my son to sea with as little mathematics and navigation as I had when I went."

All three children were entranced by the sailormen, and quickly learned to tie bowlines, grannies, clove hitches, half-hitches, sheepshanks, lashing-eyes, and Georges even learned the four strand crown sinnet around a core. It was a fair glorious time. They sailed about the lake in Georges' little boat, and Jack was delighted to see that all three could sniff for the breeze, and handle the rudder to some advantage, and that all three were proficient swimmers.

They made kites, and Jack taught Georges and the girls to recognize the effects of the varying winds, at varying altitudes, intensities, and angles, on the flight speed, maneuverability, and direction. They studied the effects of different lengths of tail on the kites, and different degrees of suppleness of the struts, and it was heartily gratifying to see the attentiveness with which Georges studied the matter, gnawing at his lip, his fair brow knotted with concentration.

The children were a merry lot, much given to humor, much of which was incomprehensible to Jack, such as their much-repeated litany of "I know a man with one leg named Dray. Prithee, what's the name of his other leg? Apparently it is Bray." Jack didn't follow the thinking, but was pleased with their laughter at it, and at some similar jape concerning a whimsical pig with wings.

Sophie, too, was a joy to be around. She looked as radiantly lovely as ever; nay, more so. She was ever of good cheer, and hardly blamed him at all for the debacle of the roof more than three times a day. Knowing that he would be leaving soon, and that the trip to the coast of the New World would be a long one, even the dowager Williams held her cruel, acid tongue on occasion.

All in all, it was a golden week, indeed, a respite from the burdens of command which would soon resume. He disciplined the children not at all this week; they required little, Sophie having raised them right properly, and what was needed was accomplished with frowns and gentle bellows rather than birch twigs. Once, when Fancy, upon being denied a treat called the dowager Williams "a gleet-faced yeasty goddammed gut-griping *poule*," he found it necessary to admonish her not to say "goddammed" because it weren't genteel, but on the whole, his brief stay at home was as halcyonic as any interlude had ever been. Nights, they made glorious fun music; Jack on his violin, Sophie coaxing vaguely soggy, sloshing sounds from her waterlogged piano ("it'll suit out fine when the sounding board dries a bit," Jack assured her, fondly running his hands over his beloved violin, caressing its scroll, pegs, neck, fingerboard, waist, tailpiece, and chinboard with genuine affection); Georges blowing on a horn at intermittent intervals unrelated to the themes explored by the adults, and Fancy and Carlotta tootling merrily on flutes, their intervals less intermittent but no less unrelated. Georges trundled out a viola da gamba; that stringed instrument somewhat of the viol family, but held between the knees (hence the name, literally viol for the leg), with approximately the range of the 'cello, which he had found in the acherontic recesses of Jack's father's house and had wheedled from his grandfather. Together they tried to coax some tunes of note from the ancient instrument. Jack found it peculiar in tone, and although he very much enjoyed his son's interest and appreciation for music, for himself, he much preferred sawing on his violin. Georges sang them a fine song about black puddings in his warbling, poorly accented French:

Préparez des oignons, hachés menus, menus,
Qu'avec autant de lard sur un feu doux l'on passe,
Les tournant tant, qu'ils soient d'un blond devenus,
Et que leur doux arome envahisse l'espace...
Mêlez le tout au sang, puis, bien assonnez,
De sel, poivre et muscade, ainsi que des épices;
Un verre de Cognac; après: vous entonnez
Dans les boyaux de porc, dont l'un des orifices
Est d'avance fermé, et dès qu'ils sont remplis,
Ficelez l'autre bout, et dans l'eau frémissante
Plongez tous les boudins! Ces travaux accomplis,
Egouttez-les après vingt minutes d'attente.[4]

---

[4]   Chop the onions, finely, finely
   Toss them in an equal amount of fat on a low fire, (NOTE: fry onions in hog's fat and lard, mixed)
   Stirring them, until they are a beautiful golden colour,
   And their fragrance pervades all around...
   Blend them with pig's blood, then season well with (NOTE: use a quart of blood, with two ounces of cream)
   Salt, pepper, nutmeg and spices;
   A glass of brandy; and then you stuff the mixture
   Into the pig's intestine, one end of which   (NOTE: stuff loosely, as mixture will expand in cooking)
   Has previously been sealed. As soon as this is filled,
   Tie up the other end and into the simmering water
   Plunge the black pudding! Once this is done,
   Give them twenty minutes, and then drain.
                           Written by Achille Ozanne

Diana had returned from a visit to her friends in France, and described the lovely streets of Paris to Stephen with a rueful smile. She and Stephen rode often; she on a fine Arabian stallion, and Stephen gamely lagging behind on a small, decrepit donkey, holding his daughter, the sweet Bridget in front of him, where she could pet the donkey's ears as they rode. Bridget could speak clearly now, and prattled gaily to her father in several languages, including one of her own invention. Stephen described to her the sixteen auricularis muscles in the ear of a horse, which enables the ear to rotate a full hundred and eighty degrees; Bridget in turn pointed out various frogs and toads of her acquaintance as they passed, distinguishing them by their teeth in the frogs, and the absence of teeth in the toads. Stephen adored her to the heavens, and sent praises and thanks to all his saints for the blessings of the child. He and Diana sat up late every night, dabbling with laudanum, smoking opium, and shooting smack.

Stephen went to visit Blaine. They spoke from teatime into the wee hours of the morning, about everything and nothing, as is often the case with old friends and fellow naturalists. They discussed aspects of the *mammalia* they had seen; placental, marsupial, and monotreme; drifting to the *aves*, and their toothless, horny beaks, large pectorals, and hollow skeletons; and thence to the *herpeton*, both reptilia and amphibia. They spoke of the pinnepids, the coelacanths, and the strange behaviours of the giant squid. Of *insectum* and *araneae* they spoke not at all, having already said everything that could <u>possibly</u> be said of such classes previously over the years of their enduring friendship.

"And here's a *Pediculus humanus capitis* I've been saving for Mr. Banks. Would you be so kind as to convey it to him, as I'll not see him before I leave?"

Blaine accepted the louse with good will. Stephen had delivered so very many lice into Mr. Banks' care, who Blaine knew well discarded all of them; but there was an inherent courtesy in him to not speak of the matter.

"And please give my dear love to his children, Jane and Michael Banks," Stephen went on. Blaine merely bowed his head kindly. Banks had no children, never had; Jane and Michael were of another Banks family, to be sure.

They touched only briefly on the primary reason for the meeting. "There are planned three invasions of the Colonies," Blaine whispered. "Niagara, Lake Champlain, and New Orleans. The Americans will fight bitterly for Lake Champlain—it's their Great Lake, you know. You must set up diversions at two points: the dissident Maryland farmers may be ripe for rebellion, as they would like to sell their foul tobacco products to our youth. And the Creek Indians in the Southeasternmost area have been sore abused by the Colonists, and may be induced to uprise."

"I am not familiar with the Creek," Stephen replied. "I am reasonably fluent in Navajo sign language, of course, and I believe it may have bearing on our dirty little business, yours and mine, at some time." He paused. "I have no facility in the Muskogean language; however, many of the words are similar to the Japanese language, which I comprehend, however poorly. But I shall endeavor to work with the Creeks, and shall do my best in both Maryland and Florida."

"You might also do well to talk to Chief Tecumseh, of the Shawnee," Blaine went on. "He fought on our side at Fort Malden, on the Detroit River, and was decisive in the capture of Detroit, and the capture of thousands of Colonial soldiers."

"I've heard of him," Nattering interjected. "But I'd heard him referred to as Tikamthe. Didn't he also help General Procter in Ohio?"

"Yes," said Blaine, "It seems no-one on that continent can even spell his own name right, whether white or red of complexion; but although the Shawnee chief was instrumental in intercepting and, I add, destroying a brigade of Kentuckians coming to relieve the fort, they never did take the Ohio fort."

"I shall make contact with Tikamthe as soon as I arrive. It shall be my highest priority," Nattering said slowly.

They broke up, and Stephen shuffled home, his yellow, scaly eyes taking in the shadowy figures watching him but not accosting him.

Back at Cedargrove Cottage, they hunted one day; Jack, Georges, Stephen, Aktaeon the groundskeeper, and Bess, the old hunting dog. Stephen was always somewhat reluctant to hunt with Captain Audibly; Jack usually carried his gun at the full-cock, and rarely bothered to carefully aim, but they saw glorious flights of fowl of every description, and brought home game enough to not only feed their own ravenous appetites, but to stock the larder for some time to come, as well. Jack did not ask about the covert portion of Stephen's mission, gliding over it with a knowing touch to his side of his nose and the remark that "*Candela* is the Latin for a candle."

While they were out, Sophie sat quietly sewing. Little Mr. Maloney, the smallest midshipman, edged up to speak to her, smiling shyly. "Begging your pardon, ma'am," he stuttered. "I've quite torn my only pair of stockings, and the Captain likes us to look so nice on board ship. D'ye suppose you might help me by mending them for me?" He gave her his most winsome smile, hanging his head.

Sophie smiled on him kindly. "Captain Audibly is a capital darner," she said brightly. "I'll ask him when he returns, and I know he'll be delighted to do it for you. He's such a sweet man. Don't be so alarmed! He's quite good at it—he won't tear your stockings!"

Mr. Maloney ran away from her in terror. Although he was certain that she was funning with him and would not, in fact, report his request, he was not at all surprised to find an enormous bundle of darning and mending waiting for him when Captain Audibly returned from the hunt, including every garment Dr. Nattering owned, save what he was wearing, which would be provided to Mr. Maloney the next day.

Jack spent a morning with Georges, absently munching a ham, his favorite snack, and working Georges' lessons, trying to impart to him of the need for numbers before joining a ship's company. "From the length and breadth of the ship is gained the main mast's length, as well as that of all the other masts. The main masts of small ships are to be three times as long as the ship is in breadth. So if a ship is twenty-five foot broad, what must her mast be?" Georges stared at him blankly, as if he'd spoken in Malay. "Come, Georges," Jack urged. "For greater ships, add the breadth to the length, and to that the half breadth, which sum shall be divided by five, and the quotient is the number of yards. So therefore, if the ship is thirty-five foot broad... " He tailed off, Georges nodding his head gently and sucking on his thumb.

Jack let the boy sleep, talking on to himself, "And the main yard is to be 2/3 and 1/12 of the main mast... "

"Seventy-five feet," whispered little Bridget, unheard, at the keyhole. "Twenty-three meters. *Vint-i-tres*," she repeated in Catalan.

Some of the people from the region came by from time to time during the week, to pay respects, or to beg favors. Jack was reluctant to take their young sons and nephews onto his ship as boys ("squeakers," as they were called, or "younkers," after the Anglicized name of the city in New York Colony that had had such a surge of young'uns born nine months after the *Aghast*, under Audibly, had last been to that city). A complement of youngsters required a schoolmaster to tend to their education, a parson to see to their moral comportment, a seamstress (or bosun) to handle their mending and ironing, and a nanny (or bosun's mate) to tuck them at nights and to oversee their upbringing. It takes a gunroom to raise a child. He was especially loath to take on his bastard sons of the area, in deference to Sophie's sensibilities; he preferred to refer them to the ships captained by his friends, and to take on their own bastard sons in return if necessary; but ships' boys were never of much use to a ship, except perhaps as ballast. Dr. Nattering had once informed him that to strengthen a Damascus sword, the blade was plunged into a slave; perhaps squeakers could be put to similar useful function, but he would not do so in any ship he commanded.

Mr. Blabbington visited with Sophie while she sat brushing the Captain's uniform.

"Begging your pardon, ma'am," he winced. "I don't care to whine, but I've got a most severe stomach-ache, and I was hoping you might hold my hand for a moment to ease it?" He smiled at her bravely, hopefully.

"You poor little lad," she cooed sweetly. "I know just the thing. Whenever Fancy or Carlotta or Georges have stomachaches, Captain Audibly rubs their tummies to make it feel better. I'll run along and fetch him, and I'm sure he'll be glad to give you comfort."

Mr. Blabbington stared, horror-fixed. Sophie stood and headed for the door. Mr. Blabbington screeched something incomprehensible, and fled. "Don't be afraid, Mr. Blabbington," Sophie called out after him. "He won't hurt you. He's the very gentlest man, as I'm sure you know."

Sophie was disconsolate at how soon Jack would be leaving - only two more days; one of which would be much taken up with the packing of his chest and dunnage and the next with his final preparations and departure. America seemed a world away, and the journey would be long and tedious.

"You shan't be far from my mind, ever," she said to him sadly. "You shan't be far."

He considered her remark. He began to chuckle, and his chuckles turned to guffaws, his eyes starting to stream and his face reddening to a bright scarlet as he bellowed and gasped. She looked at him in alarm. He was struggling to say something, but the words wouldn't come out through his uproarious laughter. Sophie smiled patiently, and waited him out. She had seen his attempts at wit before, and although it warmed the very cockles of her heart to see him happy, she was almost always at a loss when his remark finally emerged. She looked helplessly at Stephen, but medical skills were of no use in extracting words from a self-inflicted hysterical frame of mind, so they both stood back and allowed his mirth to ebb.

"Thirty-five har! Har! Har!" he got out.

They stared.

"Har, har, hardy, har, har!" he wheezed. "Not far! Not far!"

They stared.

Finally, he got it all out. "To Scilly is thirty-five leagues!" he roared, suffused with laughter.

Sophie and Stephen waited, but no more emerged, and gradually, the Abderian mood subsided.

* * *

"If I'd smoked marijuana, I should have laughed really loud at that one," Stephen reflected to Sophie, later. "You shan't. You shan't. How far."

* * *

Too quickly, the remaining days passed, and Jack and Stephen were ready to set off. The men of *Aghast* had already left the previous day. Jack hugged and kissed the little girls, gave Georges a manly clap on the shoulder, and kissed Sophie tenderly.

"*Volo, non valeo,*" Stephen uttered dully from under the post-chaise.

"I've heard the expression from my cousin in the Colonies," the driver volunteered to Jack Audibly. They mean it to say, "Help. I've fallen, and I can't get up."[5]

Sighing, Jack hoisted Stephen, and slung him into the post-chaise, looping his ankles and wrists seven times around with fine white hemp. And under the brightest of blue skies, they set off for Portsmouth, the *Aghast*, and the eastern coast of the American colonies, as the clouds billowed, pillowed overhead.

---

5   Ed. Note: Actual meaning: I am willing, but unable.

7

"Jack Audibly's snoring," Stephen mused, "has all the classical ingredients of a great work of art—simplicity, complexity, and texture. So why does it grate on me so? Faith, and I'd rather hear Solieri butcher a Mozart quartet than hear this discordance—like sweet bells, jangled, out of tune and harsh." He wondered if there was connection between the Captain's ability to produce such a clangorous charivari when he was asleep, and his difficulty in playing chamber music with musically-minded players when he was awake—"above the pitch, out of tune, and off the hinges," as Rabelais so well put it.

The thoughts of music reminded him of a question he wanted to explore with Jack, some night at sea. Stephen had long believed that the end of Bach's Fifth Brandenburg Concerto's first movement, the harpsichord cadenza, sounded as though everyone was trying to race through it; but when played slowly, as Stephen picked it out on his 'cello, it was quite elegant, lyrical. Stephen had heard P.D.Q. Locatelli play it slowly, but that was more because he lacked the technical virtuosity to keep pace with it. Maybe, Stephen mused, that was why everyone else played it so fast, to prove that they were not P.D.Q. Locatelli?

The journey was tedious, but mercifully smooth; few bumps, no tumbles. They arrived at Portsmouth, and Jack came awake instantly the air changed to a salt-sea tinged breeze. He dumped Stephen unceremoniously on the ground outside the post-chaise, warning him to watch for the *bannière de partance* at the most regular half-hourly intervals.

Stephen cocked a pale eyebrow at him. "Do you now speak French, for all love?"

Jack grinned. "It's the language they speak in heaven," he said, happy to have evoked such pleasant notice of his linguistic coup.

He discreetly signaled for Mr. Calumny, midshipman, and told him in no uncertain terms to keep the Doctor within eyesight at all times, wherever he might wander through woods and fields, and to get him onto the ship when the Blue Peter flew, even if it meant carrying him forcibly from whatever bird or bug he might be examining.

"Aye, aye, Captain," said Calumny smartly, and set off at a trot, a very fast trot indeed, as the Doctor was able to set a surprisingly rapid pace when there was a possibility of a bird to be seen.

Before Captain Audibly had gone a dozen steps, however, he was hailed by a joyously familiar voice. "Yo! Jack! Yo ho ho Jack!"

It was his old boyhood friend, Captain Heneage Dunderhead, Captain of the *Orion* (74).

"Hen, you rapacious rapscallion! How delighted I am to see you!" They strolled together to the Nelson Arms, a nearby tavern, where they ate stews made of various nondescript animals of indeterminate kill dates, braised lamb clone,[6] vegetables steam-

---

6   Braised Lamb Clone a l'Audibly:
     8 servings: or Captain Audibly and one other:

     1/2 cup olive oil
     1 cloned lamb, dressed, cut into large chunks
     4 pounds bacon or fatback
     3 large onions, chopped
     2 heads garlic, minced
     6 pounds tomatoes, cut up
     3 bottles red wine
     pinch of mint
     3 dead rats (optional)
     2 pounds ships biscuit, weevils removed (2 slices of torn-up white bread may
         be substituted

Heat oil in the copper over medium-high heat. Add lamb and bacon and cook until brown, turning occasionally, about 15 minutes.

Transfer lamb off the flame. Add onion and garlic to pan and saute until softened, about 3 minutes. Return lamb to pan, add tomatoes, wine, and mint. Cover and

boiled an unconscionable period of time, puddings, all washed down with four bottles of wine. For dessert, they munched on chunks of suet. Over brandy, Heneage described his battles against the French and his adventures of the past several months; Jack described his battle against the Cedargrove flood of '14; feeling a bit hipped at not having more to report, he recounted his meeting with Admiral Nelson, some years past. When he'd gotten to the part about "He looked directly at me, with his steady brown eyes, and said 'You goddam fat clumsy lobscouse—you've quite spilt the salt.' But he said it in so kindly a manner that I shall never forget his goodness," Dunderhead looked away, embarrassed. He'd already heard the tale, of course, dozens of times—Jack never tired of telling it—but Dunderhead had heard it quite differently from others who had been present at the dinner. It had not been salt that the young lieutenant had spilt on the Lord Admiral's snowy white pants, but a scalding serving dish filled with oleaginous bourguignonne, and neither the Admiral's remark nor his manner had been as kindly as Audibly remembered them.

"Did you say 'brown eyes?'" Dunderhead asked. "I saw a portrait of him by Guy Head, and I was struck by his shockingly blue eyes."

"No," said Jack firmly. "I remember them well—definitely brown, Vandyke brown. I suspect that they looked blue in the study you saw because his blind right eye is occasionally of a milky cast; perhaps that is how the artist saw him."

"Odd," muttered Dunderhead. "Have you ever encountered Lady Emma Hamilton? Her eyes are certainly brown."

"I had the pleasure only briefly, two years after the Battle of the Nile. And they certainly were lovely, limpid, cocoa brown, to be sure. I remember them quite clearly."

"And yet," said Dunderhead, thoughtfully, "young Horatia Nelson Hamilton has bright turquoise eyes—as bright turquoise as

---

simmer for about 2 hours, until tender. (NOTE: For London-style, simmer an additional two hours). Add dead rats during last 15 minutes. Add salt and pepper to taste. To thicken, add ships biscuit or bread and simmer, uncovered, until proper consistency.

your own!" He stopped speaking abruptly. Audibly was lost in his own thoughts.

After a pause, Heneage described in the most intimate detail his conquests of various and sundry women from London to India and everywhere in between in both directions ("a girl in every port, and a port in every girl," he guffawed coarsely); Jack mentioned the minor misunderstanding between himself and Admiral Tarte.

"Tarte!" roared Heneage. "I've not only doffed the old girl as often as most other Royal Naval officers have, but I've also enjoyed his three daughters, six nieces, and all his several mistresses these past seventeen years!"

"I see," said Audibly.

"And his four sons, too," said Dunderhead, that amiable fellow. "Alas, the poor admiral has no nephews. But if the good Lord in heaven above should favor him with a grandson, aaach, I should be very pleased, indeed. Nothing could please me more. I wish him and his sons and daughters the very greatest joy and fertility in the world."

Jack described the scrubulous nature of Captain Picard in absquatulating with Mr. Mason, and asked if Dunderhead knew of any ship's carpenter to be had.

"Carpenter. That's a tough one. Didn't you sail with Chips Hadley?"

Jack shivered. Chips had had his head lopped off by the Dyaks, those savage aborigines, a most regrettable incident, carpenters being so hard to replace. Damn them for the inconvenience. Jack Audibly sincerely hoped that their Dyak ampallangs were as inconvenient to them as the loss of his carpenter was to him.

"Then what about Mr. Beattey?" Dunderhead asked.

"Even more regrettable," Jack replied. "Mr. Beattey had gotten himself mixed up with a Mr. Bentley, a mere misunderstanding, *lapsus linguae*, the names being so similar; but with fatal consequences—Beattey had been killed in a duel with a man Bentley had royally cuckolded."

"Sad, wery, wery sad," sighed Dunderhead. "I'm afraid I can't serve you on this."

"And you'll not believe the discussion I had with my particular friend, Stephen Nattering, on the subject," Jack frothed. "After all the years he's been sailing with me, and I've tried my level best to instruct him in the handling of a ship at sea, and he asked me only this morning why I shouldn't just sail on without a carpenter on board. As if he himself could hammer a nail if needed, if shown a hundred times over which end to hit, and with which end of the hammer!"

"I wonder at Nattering at times," Dunderhead muttered. "I've seen him myself to fall off from chairs under the effort of buttering his crumpets, and on dry land, too. And yet, I hear he's a capital surgeon. God forfend he should ever attend me in one of my toothaches, but I'm told the men idolize him."

"He's a really capital physician when not under the narcotic influence," Jack responded. "And he's capital company, as well. He plays a grand 'cello, and he knows so very much about birds, and insects, and natural philosophy of all sorts. And you would not credit what he did with a hammered out three-shilling piece and Mr. Lackey's whirleygigs." His voice tailed off, as he recalled the carpenter discussion of this morning. Stephen had indeed asked the question of sailing without a carpenter. After determining by piercing stare that he was not being made game of, Jack had explained to him the carpenter's duties and responsibilities. Stephen had nodded gravely, wondered whether the boatswain, or 'bosun' as he had heard him termed, couldn't serve just as well, and proceeded apace into a description of a most interesting arachnid he had seen... And without so much as a *vertamur ad melliora*, Jack thought sadly.

"Still," Jack reflected to himself, "I wouldn't lose the dear man's friendship for all the best carpenters of the world."

They diagrammed past battles in beer on the table board, and drank the health of everyone they knew. They noted with annoyance a party of drunken, boisterous seaman at the tavern singing *ça ira*, one of whom had yawned with considerable technicolour, staining Captain Audibly's formerly highly spit-polished black leather boots; but the man had quite passed out under the table immediately thereafter, so there was no opportunity for biting remark. Jack noticed with displeasure that his own coxswain and steward were among the revelers. His steward would regret the incident the next day, when he received his captain's boots.

"Come, friend, a small *deoch an doris* with you," said Dunderhead, and then Jack and Heneage Dunderhead parted at three in the morning; Hen staggering drunkenly to the *Orion*, assisted by his boatswain; and Jack, not drunk by naval standards, being still able to grasp his throbbing head between his two arms, to respire without assistance, and to curse the French, made his way to the *Aghast*. There was a nip in the air now, and he hugged his boatcloak around his broad chest, glancing at the pre-dawn sky apprehensively, shivering at the prospect of another long, possibly fruitless voyage. It had been hours since he'd seen Sophie, and he looked around hopefully for one of the young women usually to be found in proximity to the Portsmouth docks; but they had all either found employment for the evening already, or had retired to... to wherever it was they retired to. He wished he knew. As his aspirations and member diminished, the stars above did likewise. It was still winter in England, and he heard Sirocco and Boreas bursting forth from the iron gates; all the winds at war.

8

After two hours sleep, Jack Audibly awakened refreshed and perfectly alert. Although he had boarded on the larboard side when he arrived, due to modesty over his somewhat inebriated condition, all hands knew, of course, that he was onboard, and were cleaned and ready for muster. Even before inspection, he began immediately spewing his customary string of aischrolatreia, intending to set sail that very even-tide, and was pleased to see that the master, Mr. Aeolos, was industriously bent over a neat set of charts, smiling as he studied them, and his first lieutenant, Tom Pushings, had already seen to the ship's lading, provisioning, and rigging. The *Aghast* having already been fitted out, Pushings had carefully examined her sails, yards, ropes, pulleys, anchors, and all riggings, and determined everything to be shipshape; he had also seen to her provisions and stores, her ballast, had properly stowed the hold; in short, he had done what he was supposed to have done, as it was expected that he should have done, and had done so without the usual running commentary on the men, their heritage, descendence, and other undistinguishing characteristics so usually commented upon in such times. Actually, Captain Audibly rarely spoke bawdy himself; he only used the "f"-word as an interjection or an adjective; never as a verb and rarely as a noun.

Captain Audibly was less pleased when he clapped his eyes upon his coxswain, Baretta Blondin. Blondin was helping the boatswain and his mates with their cordage and rigging and anchors and canvas, but he had a companion with him; the sot that had befouled the captain's boots the previous evening. This worthy touched his knuckle to his forehead and ramrodded himself to attention when the captain appeared. Captain Audibly nodded for Blondin to speak.

"With permission, sir, may I present my good friend, Mjollnir, former carpenter of the frigate *Frolic*, which was..." here he dropped his voice to a hoarse whisper, "taken," he glanced around to see if his unseemly word had been overheard, "by the Americans in the *Wasp* in October, '12. If we don't yet have a carpenter, I thought you might like to meet him..." Blondin saw the captain frown, and promptly clamped his mouth shut, reinforcing it by holding his mouth with both his hands, lowering his head and peeking upwards at the Captain.

Jack looked crossly at Mjollnir, but quickly reassessed his position. "Have ye' your warrant?" he asked gruffly.

"Aye, aye, sir," Mjollnir said right smartly, touching his hand to forehead again, while reaching into his shirt for the precious paper. "And it's right properly signed and sealed, too," he added.

"Let me see your tools," Jack asked, somewhat less gruffly. Mjollnir seemed to have sobered up a considerable notch, although he still squinted something fierce in the bright, rising sunlight. Jack edged a step to his side, causing Mjollnir to turn toward him and in doing so, to have the fullest sun in his face. Mjollnir produced his tools, and Jack noted with approbation that they were clean and sharp, and that the man was well equipped for his trade.

"See him signed in," Jack told Mr. Pushings. He looked back to Mjollnir, now clearly uncomfortable in the rapidly increasing sunglare of the morning, trying not to shield his eyes with his hand, but squinting and streaming. "How long were you off America?" Jack asked.

"Two months," Mjollnir replied, "and not a happy time it was. They don't fight right, you know, they don't hold a formation at all, but they got us anyway, blamed if I knew how it come about. And nights, when we sometimes slipped up onto their shores for a bite and a nip..." He stopped himself short. "For a bite to eat, and they can't brew a decent tea at all, nor yet coffee neither, and you can't understand a word they say. I've known them to serve tea leaves with sugar and discard the water the leaves had been boiled in. I have kin there, but they can't hold their liquor, or spell..." But Captain Audibly was striding away, bellowing orders as he went, for the re-stowing and re-reefing and re-everything that fell under his eye.

"A moment, Mr. Mjollnir, if you please," Jack stepped back as Mjollnir started to avert his eyes from the sun. Mjollnir snapped a salute. "Quillick!" Jack bellowed. "Quillick, where the bloody h___ are you, you golter-yeded gawpsheet?!"

"Which I'm coming, ain't I?" Quillick whined as he crept forward, carrying the captain's coffee proffered in both hands.

"Oooh," Mr. Dan Rowan whispered to Mr. Richard Martin. "That's a good'un. Golter-yeded gawpsheet. How d'ye spell that, d'ye know?"

"Quillick!" Jack roared in his ear when he got close, at full blast, so as to be heard over the wavelet gently lapping against the unmoving ship. "Ask Mr. Mjollnir to be most kind enough and to wipe down my boots, if he would. They're as speckled as a Frenchman's pillow! D'ye hear me, Quillick?"

The ship prepared to weigh, and the Blue Peter flew. From all along the shore, those libertymen who had not been involved in the preparations streamed toward the *Aghast.* Many were sad to leave home and hearth, or apprehensive about committing themselves to another six or twelve months of subjugation to rules, regulations, startings, floggings, mastings, and the constant buggery, but every man jack among them was a volunteer, and most were glad to return to what they were used to, a regular life with no changes of any kind, no mad interference with the one hot square meal per day in a steady succession of macaroni and cheese and sushi on Mondays, ratwurst and sushi on Tuesdays, catsup sandwiches (recently reclassified as a meat by the Admiralty Board, as a cost-saving reinvention initiative) and sushi on Wednesdays, weevil stew and sushi on Thursdays, weenie-beanies and sushi on Fridays, pizza and sushi on Saturdays, and maggotburgers (the other white meat) and sushi and (joy of joys!) chocolate pudding with sprinkles and marshmallows on Sundays (except for Clumsy Dravis, who preferred ladyfingers to marshmallows, owing to dietary restrictions of a religious nature); with occasional special morsels, such as the never-to-be-forgotten sloth soup; all to be washed down in rich, flowing grog, or with a gallon of rum per man or boy; and it was only on rare occasion, when they ran out of all of the above, that they had to fall back on stir-fried tofu, raspberry yoghurt and Perrier. The men sang merrily as they rowed in, and straining, Captain Audibly was pleased to hear their cheerful voices raised in anticipation of the voyage, singing *Roast Beef of Old London*.[7]

---

7   *The Roast Beef of Old England* (Ain't It Prime Beef?)

When Mighty Roast Beef was the Englishman's Food
It ennobled our veins and enriched our Blood:
Our Soldiers were Brave and our Courtiers were Good:
Oh! The Roast Beef of Old England,
And Old English Roast Beef.

But since we have learned from all vapouring France,
To eat their Ragouts, as well as to Dance.
We are fed up with nothing but vain Complaisance,
Oh! The Roast Beef of Old England,
And Old English Roast Beef.

Our Fathers, of old, were Robust, Stout and Strong,
And kept open House, with good cheer all day long.
Which made their plump Tenants rejoice in this Song,
Oh! The Roast Beef of Old England,
And Old English Roast Beef.

But now we are dwindled, to what shall I name,
A sneaking poor Race, half begotten ... and Tame,
Who Sully those Honours that once shone in Fame,
Oh! The Roast Beef of Old England,
And Old English Roast Beef.

When good Queen Elizabeth sat on the throne
E'er Coffee and Tea and such slip-slops were known;
The World was in Terror if e'er she did frown.
Oh! The Roast Beef of Old England,
And Old English Roast Beef.

But not from every corner of Portsmouth did they so stream. The requisite thirty minutes passed, and another thirty besides; and eyes scanned the shore for a sight of Doctor Nattering, but scan the shore they did in vain. Boys scampered up the mast to the masthead, or whatever highest point they could reach, because the captain had promised sixpence to the first to raise the cry of "Doctor, she blows!" The tide flowed, the ship did not. Captain Audibly stared at the red, baize bag that held the cat-o-nine-tails, and thought grim thoughts about Mr. Calumny and Dr. Nattering both. A singularly sweet smile curled his lip at the thoughts, but quickly froze as he glanced at the sky and the sea, and at the dying tide.

Just as the tide completed its evening run, he heard a squeaking piping call of, "It's the doctor approaching the coast!" Jack glanced at the baize bag again, but heard the same voice to cry out, "No, sorry, it was just a very small horse." Jack sighed.

Again the cry pitched out, "Doctor, ahoy!" Again it was followed by a soft, "Sorry. It's yet another horse."

"Will somebody please yank that child down from the topgallant mast!" Jack started to call out, but even before the words had left his lips, a body hurtled past and smashed into the quarterdeck beside him, splattering something fierce. Jack stared. It was the squeaker, one of the Portsmouth boys, Mr. Icarus, who had just joined as servant in hopes of someday becoming a seaman. "Moppers!" Jack called loudly, and a crew sprang to the quarterdeck to clean the mess.

The tide ebbed, and reversed itself. Jack stared longingly at the baize bag, and heard soft, stumbling footsteps behind him on the holy quarterdeck.

In those days, if Fleets did presume on the Main,
They seldom, or never, returned back again,
As witness, the Vaunting Armada of Spain.
Oh! The Roast Beef of Old England,
And Old English Roast Beef.

"Peekaboo," warbled Stephen. "Are you surprised to see me, my dear? Sure, and I've been on board for hours. I wanted to see if you'd wait for me."

"Calumny!" shrieked Captain Audibly, in a voice usually reserved for direst emergency or singing in Church.

Calumny edged forward, his hands and mouth bound with surgeon's adhesive tape. Jack ripped the tape off with an abrupt jerk.

"Ouch, that stings!" cried Calumny. "And the Doctor said he'd sew my lips shut if I let on that he wuz here. He put one over on you, sir, if I may make so bold!"

Captain Audibly glared at Calumny so hard as to make the youth's blood run cold. And run it would, soon, on the grate, too. Calumny slunk away, muttering under his breath, "Ain't that prime, though. And when it suits him, he can board the ship with nary a splash, nor a wet foot, neither."

"I beg you will take notice, Captain, that I actually was come aboard more than twenty-four minutes before I was obligated to do so; I desire that this will be taken into account and credited to me should ever I be untimely in the future," Stephen said, *integer vitae*, innocent, blameless, even commendable, but unable to conceal a hint of a sly smirk.

The officers who were required to be on the deck snuck to the most distant reaches they could attain. Jack looked at Stephen with blood in his eyes. Stephen gazed back on Jack, quizzically. "Sure, and you're not angry with me, are you?" he asked incredulously.

Jack couldn't bring himself to speak. He strove mightily to control his anger. Normally slow to anger, and quick to forgive, he was now shaking in his attempt to restrain from throttling his very best friend bodily.

"And I have important news to impart, too," Stephen began.

Jack burned. "What, pray, is it this time? Is it a beetle? A bug? Some goddamned louse again?" He glared, and added under his voice, "*nulliu filius*."

Stephen looked dismayed. "Sure, and it concerns our mission, too. But if you're going to be so frampold, in such a snit, I'd just as soon not tell you just tonight. It will certainly keep until tomorrow."

Jack's face grew red, and he shook violently; but got himself under control. "Pray," he said sweetly, "and what is it about our voyage that you've to say, and is it relevant to the fact that we've quite missed the tide, and won't be able to sail for another twelve hours, unless you'd like to singlehandedly wear the ship out of the harbor? I've some spare sets of oars, too, as you're bound to lose the first dozen you lay your damned hands upon."

Quillick whispered loudly to Playce, "Which the doctor has gone and done it this time, costing the Captain his tide. Doctor M is the best at your liver and bunions, but when it comes to a ship, he doesn't know his oars from his elbow."

"And what are we losing not a minute for, anyway?" Stephen asked. "Surely the war will still be going on if we get to America twelve hours later, won't it really?"

"I've my orders, not that you'd understand such a thing," Jack replied. "And when a ship goes to battle, there's oft-times not a moment to be lost, or haven't you ever even heard the expression to stick between your ears until now?"

Stephen looked sad. "I believe I have heard the term well spoken of in the past. However, right now, for all the world, you remind me of that fellow Buonaparte, who said to his aide in 1803 'Go, sir, gallop, and don't forget that the world was made in six days. You can ask me for anything you like, except time.' I'm sorry to say this, Jack, but you sound for all the world like that 'un. I'm going to bed now, as I've had quite a busy day of it, while you've just been lollygagging about, having yourself a grand time on this boat. And by the by, I'll mention that I today did you a kindness, in truth. I had occasion to cross paths with Admiral Cochrane in a corridor, and I put in as kindly a word for you as ever I have; told him you were an excellent sailorman, and could even tell starboard from larboard with nary a glance toward the figurehead."

Stephen considered Jack Audibly's face with concern. It was red, far too red for Dr. Nattering's professional judgment. He regretted in deeply, but duty being what it was, he would necessarily bring himself to bleed the Captain—not that he would raise the issue now, of course—but perhaps tomorrow, certainly no later than the next day, in good conscience, it would have to be done. He sighed. Captain Audibly hated to be bled. For a man who would face the imminent prospect of death without pause when duty called, he was, not to put too fine a point on it, afraid—yes, afraid—of the wee little lancet, often accusing Dr. Nattering of confusing him for Louis XIII. But cowardice would not sway the doctor from his professional responsibility. He would be duty-bound to bleed the captain, whose face was still beet-red. In fact, he reflected, if the captain persisted in this unfortunate fury, which was not at all good for his liver, that poor overworked organ, Stephen would be forced to purge him as well.

Jack started to brindle to Stephen's use of the word "boat," but decided to fight just the one battle at a time; he had previously enjoined Stephen against calling the *Victory* "a boat," and didn't care to reopen the subject. He started to reply, but bit back the comment, although it took all his effort to do so.

"Before I turn in, however," Stephen paused, "I wonder if we shouldn't have some toasted cheese together. I haven't supped yet..." He saw Jack's furious face, and walked away, dejected, but savoring his moral advantage.

9

Following a good night's sleep and his first breakfast of the day, Jack Audibly's natural affability had returned. (Jack generally took his first breakfast before Stephen awoke, as Stephen usually managed to glop up the sides of the honeyjar). The ship sailed with the first of the tide, the Highlanders weighing anchor while the Orkneymen were on the forecastle, gathered around their leader, Mack the Mackerel. Tom Pushings gave the orders with barely a hint of blasphemy, the bosun piped them in the shorthand of the sea, and the hands on the forecastle instantly clapped on to the falls, Mack the Mackerel at their head.

A slight pause, and then, throwing his weight on the rope, he sang out:

"A wop bop a looma, a wop bop bop"
followed by his mates in perfect unison, singing:

"Mairzy doats and dozey doats and liddle lambsy divey."

They sang on a scale unknown at the time, with intervals no human had ever sung before, and the last line, a falsetto shriek as the blocks clashed together and someone's finger sheared off, quite unnerved Captain Audibly.

"Mr. Pushings," he said. "I'm not quite pleased with the foretopsailyard; pray let it be eased off and settled a trifle more snugly. I should like to see the man with nine fingers to do it, if you please."

He turned to Stephen, who had just stumbled on deck. "Would you care to observe the maneuver?"

Stephen stifled a groan, and set his face into a rictus of a smile. "Nothing would please me more. My nipples are erect to see a sail furled or birled or hurled."

When they had cleared the crowded harbor, and the ship was settling down to its usual routine, Captain Audibly sat for a light second breakfast with Dr. Stephen Nattering, and over fresh orange juice, toasted soft bread liberally spread with Sophie's excellent plum preserves, rashers of bacon, dozens of eggs, and frosted flakes, Stephen described the discouraging bit of news he had learned the previous day. He looked around cautiously for Quillick, but the steward was nowhere in sight. Nonetheless, he lowered his voice to tell Jack some of his primary mission for the voyage, chief of which was his meeting with Chief Tecumseh of the Shawnee; unfortunately, Tecumseh has been killed just two weeks ago.

"I see," said Jack, staring incredulously at his hands. They were as sticky as a Spaniard's shirtfront, his fingers were tacky, his coffee mug was sticking to his coatsleeve. His morning correspondence and bills were covered with honey. He glanced at Stephen, who was placidly munching on a pancake. "That changes things considerably, does it not? Are we still to go?"

"No change, and it's to America that we'll be sailing, despite the untimely death of this greatest of American heroes." He paused, searching for the proper phrase. "Wind and tide permitting." Reflecting on the contretemps of the previous evening, he hastened to add, "Note that had we left twelve hours sooner, it would not have affected my rendezvous with Tecumseh in any event, even had we cracked an egg till all sneered again. He had been dead even before we received our several instructions; word has only just gotten to England." He paused. "But I'll have to devise a new strategy for when we arrive. Are we almost there yet, by the by? Sure and we've been on the sea all day, it seems."

Jack made no reply, stuffing his mouth instead with a chocolate cake. After he'd swallowed, and washed it down with a quart of goat's milk, he asked Stephen quietly, "What, pray tell, is in the gray sack in our cabin?"

Captain Audibly was justified in apprehension—Stephen had brought all sorts of vile and obnoxious creatures on previous voyages, and as they shared a sleeping cabin, Captain Audibly had oft-times been awakened by a vampire bat sucking at his neck, or a grizzly bear bent on wrestling him for custody of his hammock, or a louse crawling up his privates, and once, just after the taking of the *Alastor*, near Callao, by a falcon, ripping at his eyes in the dark. Audibly had nearly lost the use of that eye. He had long-standing left orders that Dr. Nattering was to be strip-searched upon boarding the ship, but he knew uneasily that Nattering had this time slipped on board unnoticed.

"Would there be any more coffee?" Stephen started to ask, employing the time-honoured trick of espionage agents of changing the subject, but it wasn't going to work this time. Jack stifled a moan, remembering the time Stephen had brought a hundred or so lemmings onto his ship to study their social patterns. It had occupied the round-the-clock attention of two boys, an able seaman, and an unusually responsible midshipman to continually rescue the horrid beasts as they hurled themselves overboard at every opportunity. Captain Audibly was further incensed when one of the boys assigned to the task produced a letter from his mother, requesting that her son remain below decks during inclement weather; this meant that the Captain himself had to jump into the frigid North Sea waters to rescue Stephen's project on occasion. (Although he refrained from complaint to Stephen, he particularly resented that he often was bitten by the creatures in the very act of saving them; and he felt aggrieved that Stephen unfailingly would berate him on such occasions for getting his hair wet on a cold night, and would inexorably purge and bleed him the next day, to prevent the sniffles). As the voyage progressed, the lemmings chose to nest in the guns, despite Captain Audibly's nightly practice firings. This led to a genuine embarrassment, as not a few French and Spanish officers had discussed the situation amongst themselves and officers of other navies whenever they got together, so that the mention of Captain Jack Audibly's name was oft-times associated with a hooting, "I've been lemminged!" in grievously insubordinate tones.

"What gray sack in our cabin?" he tried next, using the second most time-honoured trick of espionage agents, that of misunderstanding the question. "I've only a wee taupe sack."

"Prithee, what might be in the aforementioned taupe sack?" Jack persisted.

"Oh, it's only, oh, a small serpent I picked up for our amusement," Stephen replied nonchalantly.

"Ah, all right then," Jack said with some relief, thinking of the sweet music made by the serpent, an ancient coiled, bass wind instrument of wood covered with leather. His father, General Audibly, Whig extraordinaire, had had one when Jack was a boy, and he remembered playing duets with that worthy when he was himself learning to coax sound from a violin.

"And would there then be any coffee left at all?" Stephen asked quickly, again changing the subject.

"Speaking of Tecumseh's untimely demise, had you heard that LaGrange died a few months past?" Jack asked.

"D'ye mean the Frenchman who tinkered up that ridiculous calendar?" Stephen responded.

"Actually," said Jack, "he was born in Italy, and the ridiculous calendar was the least of his notions. He was probably the greatest mathematician of our time, and I am a great admirer of his. In fact, he was offered an honorary doctorate at Trinity College, but he declined the honour, of course."

"I knew he was well spoken of in some circles, but I had thought the French republican calendar to be his crowning achievement," Stephen replied.

"Certainly the calendar had its faults; it represents the worst of the Mob's pandering to those who want to turn everything topsy-turvey—no weeks, no Christian Sundays, months bearing no relation to the months of the rest of the world, and so on," Jack agreed. "Even the fool Napoleon had to abandon it eventually. I abhor innovations myself. But LaGrange understood the libration of the Moon better than anyone else. He was kind enough to write to me concerning my paper on nutation, pointing out the parts in which my thinking emulated his, and the other parts, that were perhaps mistaken."

"I'm delighted to hear of it—I had no idea," Stephen smiled. "It was certainly grand of him to do so. I shall offer a prayer for him, despite his being a senator and count of the empire."

"Yes," replied Jack somberly. "The road to heaven is paved with good inventions."[8]

"Actually, I should have thought that Messier would have been your hero in the scientific realm," said Stephen.

"Messier had some good ideas, to be sure, and I admire him greatly. I wondered sometimes, however, of his spirit of exploration. Did you know that the intention of his catalog was not so much a guide to the comets as a guide to what were not comets?"

Stephen scratched his stubble. "What do you mean by that?"

"He apparently thought he should be the only ferret to find out comets. His catalog was designed to show areas where no-one should look for comets, because he thought there weren't any there. He called such areas 'nebulae,' and didn't want anybody to report any comets in those areas, the scrub."

Stephen continued to scratch himself. "Sure, I don't know enough about him to dispute what you say, but it seems that discovering where something isn't should be a help in discovering where it might be, else. But I'm certain that you are in the right of it. No true scientist should tell other explorers where not to seek their discoveries... Ahh, that was a jolly one," he added, for Captain Audibly was by now seated on the throne of comfort. A plucky young midshipman also ventured to wish the Captain joy, but quickly vanished.

"Actually, there is one other item to discuss," Jack said, with considerable diffidence. "I hate to complain or to be difficult, though."

"Pray, tell," Stephen soothed. "Nothing could please me more than to hear out your gripings and *kvetching*."

---

8   Kate Jones, inventor.

Jack frowned, but went on. "It's the cabin which we share. I enjoy your company, of course, but I wonder if your personal items might be more cautiously placed into containers, racks, chests, shelves, and other appurtenances designed for the safekeeping and, I might add, neatness, of their contents. Not that I have any objection to slovenliness or poor personal habits myself, but it would be such a kindness to the men who clean up after you, of course."

Stephen fixed him with a reptilian glare. "I don't consider myself slovenly, or possessed of poor personal habits, you know. I prefer to refer to my heaps as 'a wondrous tolerance for ambiguity,' or 'locational despecificity.'"

Jack slunk back to the cabin and tidied Stephen's papers, wiped his knife, bottled the stool samples, disposed of obviously abandoned foodstuffs, shook out the physician's wig, and sorted Stephen's clothes into neat stacks.

After breakfast, Stephen checked on the sick-berth. There was little to be done so early in the cruise—Mr. MacMillan, the dreamer, had third degree burns about his face as usual following home leave, and there were a few hernias from weighing anchor, along with the usual number of hockogrockles and numdudgeons, but no serious illness or injuries. Dr. Nattering was pleased to see that Able Seaman Richard Gere had recovered fully from the prior voyage's somewhat painful, rather embarrassing operation, which he had implored the doctor to list in the medical log as a suprapubic cystotomy. Only one new hand was deemed physically unfit for service, to be put ashore immediately—Seaman Pudden Tame's back was so severely striped that Dr. Nattering did not believe he could survive identifying himself to yet another captain. Captain Audibly was suspicious, but did not wish to offend the doctor; he quietly whispered:

"Oh, what a tangled web we... we..."

"Cribellate?" Stephen suggested.

"Captain Audibly smiled sweetly.

"Just so."

Captain Audibly was aggrieved at losing a seemingly able-bodied man, but Dr. Nattering explained firmly that as a result of an unfortunate fist fight, the man suffered from a circumorbital haematoma, and Audibly quickly excused himself and fled from the sick-berth. Reverend Nathaniel Martinet was down with his chronic obstipation, so common to the Scottish; and Clumsy Dravis suffered to a higher degree than usual from his porraceous fluxe, but neither was cause for great concern. Quillick described his physical complaints at great length; Dr. Nattering listened attentively, and prescribed a course of pink pills, his usual remedy for menstrual cramps and similar problems of a purely psychological nature. Captain Audibly wondered at times about the pattern of grievances in the sick-berth. He had heard Dr. Nattering expound from time to time that "you get more of what you reinforce." Certainly, Nattering's sick-berths tended to have an abundance of bowel disorders, far more than Audibly had seen in other ships. He wondered if Stephen's preoccupation with same was the cause for so many reported alimentary ailments. Lost in thought, the Captain walked on the quarterdeck. All the old pattern fell into place again, and the ship's routine soon became the natural way of life once more, with its unvarying diets, the flogging of men before full daylight, the constant call for sweepers and moppers, as ship's boys fell from the masts with dismaying frequency during the early days of the cruise, the piping of all hands to witness punishments, reprimand or force-feeding of excessive quantities of grog, the ritual wet-towel fights on Mondays and Fridays, beating of the men in quarters every weekday with a certain amount of *Schadenfreude* on the part of those not beaten, mustering by divisions on Sundays, followed sometimes by the beating or flogging of the men, or worse, by Church. It was a comparatively pleasant life, for masochists, but boring on days when the grate was not rigged. Seaman Patrick Tullster took a round dozen every night the first week, for reading his books out loud nights, keeping the other sailors awake, but he was soon cured of that unfortunate tendency (although he continued to move his lips when he read).

On the first Sunday after setting out, Church was rigged, as usual, and Captain Audibly read out the Articles of War in an especially tonitrual, especially sepulchral voice, seeking to set the tone for the voyage. As usual, he skipped over number Twenty-One, but gave special emphasis to number Three: If any officer, mariner, soldier, or other person of the fleet shall display, hold, or entertain intelligence of any uncommon degree, without leave from the king's majesty, or the lord high admiral, or the commissioners for executing the office of lord high admiral, commander in chief, or his commanding officer, every such person so offending, and being thereof convicted by the sentence of a court martial, shall be punished with ostracism. When he reached Article Twenty-Nine, he cast a fierce glare on Seaman Gere, who grinned self-effacingly and shrugged.

They passed *Swiftsure* as they proceeded westward, just returned from sinking *Bene Gesserit*, Jack pointing her out proudly to Stephen. Stephen studied her with his glass. "Sure, and she's the beautiful ship of the world," he said enthusiastically. "Would she be termed a 'frigate?'"

Jack stared at Stephen with open-mouthed disbelief. Even considering other questions Stephen had asked in the past, he was utterly speechless.

"Don't fret your head, for all love," Stephen reassured him. "I'll ask Tom Pushings. I'm sure he'll know."

The men's days were so regular that they soon developed the insensibility that allowed them to holystone the decks as in their dreams, not even noticing the captain's orotund snoring eighteen inches below their ears, changes in the riggings of the ship, gales and storms, or changes in the wind whistling through the sails; shooting to intense wakefulness only at the genial swish of the red baize bag being opened; a signal that entertainment was soon to follow.

Jack's days were usually a pleasant routine. It was so regular that one day, except for the identity of the miscreant(s) to be flogged, was much the same as the other. He seldom wore boots, and frequently had his feet wet. When this occurred, he would go down to his cabin, throw his britches into a heap, and walk on the carpet in his stockings to dry them. He chose to adopt this uncomfortable expedient rather than give Quillick the trouble of assisting him to put on fresh stockings, which, from his massive girth, he could not himself conveniently effect. He spent very little time with the midshipmen in the beginning, as they were so prone to disaster, and he did not expect them to survive long enough to justify his attention. One member of the midshipmen's berth took his particular attention, however. Mr. Keating, a youth of particular beauty from East Sussex, who had naturally curly, tawny golden ringlets, small, dainty teeth, translucent skin, and the aroma of pistachio nuts about him. He had a grace and charm to him; an easy smile, and a most beguiling curve of neck, which Stephen had commented upon more than once. "He couldn't possibly be a day over eleven. Must have lied about his age," Jack mused. Jack didn't mind, of course. He had lied about his own age when going to sea at around the same age, and had lied about it again to Sophie, telling her he was only twelve, certainly no more than fourteen, years older than she. "He's lucky that his uncle, Mr. Andrews, is a most particular friend of Diana Villiers-Todd-Burton-Canning-Johnstone-Johnson-Onassis-Nattering's; I don't normally approve of such young'uns, but she persuaded me, in that special way she has of persuading men to do her bidding, to take the lad on, so he can embark on an honorable career." Jack took a special interest in the boy. He knew, of course, that Mr. Mjollnir, the carpenter, was buggering the young boys; Jack disapproved of pederasty, but took no action: *chacun a son gout*. Besides, Mjollnir was a particular friend of Mr. London, the sailmaker, and a good sailmaker was a jewel beyond desire, and Mr. London was a good one. He had always kept the sails in good repair, and his surveys and conversions of sails were reliable. During inspections, Captain Audibly had always been pleased that the sails in the storeroom were dry, preserved from vermin as well as damps and drips. A minor matter such as buggery was offensive to Jack's taste, but not worth upsetting his warranted sailmaker over.

One night, Jack sent for the boy to the quarterdeck; he appeared, nervous and jittery, expecting abuse. Jack spoke to him kindly, as he would to his own son, Georges. Jack pointed out some of the more common constellations in the night sky; Mr. Keating took a genuine interest, and learned quickly. He seemed quicker than the other boys with the special tools of the midshipmen's acquaintance—the sextant did not terrify him, as it did so many others of his age and inexperience; and he was quick with figures of single digit; an improvement over the rest of the berth, even though he was the youngest. Captain Audibly thought the lad could enjoy expectation of good future.

The days passed easily. The winds and the weather were favorable, there was ample work for all hands to be fully occupied, but not excessively so. They practiced gunnery evenings—*Beati pacifici*, murmured Stephen—the smell of the slowmatch and powder pleasant to the nostrils, and the sound of the cannons booming were as musical as any long-lost Locatelli quartet. Jack had laid in a large private stock of powder and shot, for as he usually quipped, the Navy Board had been penny wise and pounder foolish. This put him in mind of the American Benjamin Franklin's remarks to the effect that a penny saved was a penny earned was a penny taxed, so it all came out the same in the end, and he considered his funds spent on gunpowder to be invested rather than expended. Nights, the sailors would sing and dance. All the men smiled at the sight of Stephen Nattering, elbow flapping madly, doing a very creditable version of the Americans' dance "the funky chicken" with little Readey, whose face shone with sheer delight. Captain Audibly reluctantly had to forbid the marines, in their bright red-coats and shining buttons, from quickening the dance steps with shots from their pistols, American-style, as they were holing his decks something awful. Punishment was relaxed as compared to strict naval standards, as the hand-picked crew of long standing were self-disciplined to an extraordinary extent; what floggings there were occurred more for their entertainment value than from need for punishment or deterrence. Captain Audibly was not known as a hard-horse flogging captain, but he believed in the Royal Navy saw, *qui bene amat bene castigat.*

Today, however, the grate was rigged in earnest, for there were to be two floggings. The men, in a rush of high spirits, had gotten into a food fight yesterday, and had not only wasted the day's rations, but had despoiled the decks, spattered the masts, and rendered the riggings dangerously slippery. Mr. London, the sailmaker, was especially aggrieved at the staining of his lovely sails, which he had labored so long and hard to wash just the previous day. The hands were mustered, and a ripple of excitement titillated the deck, although no man dared to speak.

The first of the two to be punished, Mr. James Dillon, was stripped to the waist and lashed to the grate. He had been the first to flip the pepperoni from his pizza, still dripping with hot cheese, at Mr. Ned Flanders,[9] although there was talk that Flanders had clearly said "if you please, to <u>pass</u> me a biscuit <u>or something</u>." Dillon took his thirty strokes manfully, without a cry. His back was already heavily striped from previous lashings, not a few of which were for similar misdemeanors. His mates flung buckets of salt water on his back to soothe it, and led him back to the deck to witness the punishment of his foe.

Jack Audibly watched the flogging of Mr. Dillon with narrowed eyes. It was unseemly that he should be so silent, considering how the hands loved a boisterous, clamorous flogging as a break from their daily routine of eating, working, and sleeping. "Damned inconsiderate," he thought. A thought started to occur to him, evaporated, and returned, stronger. He held up an imperious hand to halt the progress of Mr. Dillon back to the maindeck, while he formulated a remark. He was sure he had something witty to say, but it didn't come. All eyes gawked on him, those men in the rear craning for a glimpse; ears strained toward the *mot* they knew was

---

9   Ed. Note: A distant kin to Matthew Flinders

coming, but didn't want to miss whatever it was. Gradually, he began to suffuse with chuckles. The men chuckled, too, in keen anticipation. His eyes began watering, streaming, his face went to vermilion, he began shaking all over. He started to speak in paroxysm, but it took several minutes before he could eke out, "What's the matter, Mr. Dillon? Cat got your tongue?"

The men considered this for a while. A few chuckled out of politeness, but it was clear that most didn't smoke it. They gazed at each other for a while. Mr. McMichael whispered to Mr. Milislavsky that although the Captain clearly thought his remark was funny, it wasn't quite the rip in Buonaparte's britches, and the men again turned their eyes toward Mr. Flanders.

Mr. Flanders' offense had been more serious. Not only had he flung his food in Dillon's general direction, with the accompanying splatters that had so enraged everyone in the messroom that they all joined the melee; all, that is, except Clumsy Dravis, who always sat alone at meals (except for the company of Mr. Alferd Packer and Mr. Michael Tyson) owing to the men's distrust of his anthropophagy; with projectile mashed potatoes hurling aloft and alow, the last, the very last of the fresh tomatoes being crammed into cheeks and squirted back out by the pounding of the outside of the cheeks by fist at each other,[10] whole pints of chilled fresh-squeezed lemonade being poured down the napes of men's necks; but Flanders had drawn an additional fifteen strokes for "taunting"—he had flung in the face of the young midshipman, who tried to interrupt the fight, the oft-repeated dastardly canard of the Royal Navy, "Aft the more honor, forward the better man."

Vogel, the bosun's mate, again drew the cat from its red baize bag, phlegmatically took up his stance, and as the ship reached the

---

[10] This phenomenon sorely vexed Captain Audibly when he attempted to describe it in his log. Try as he might, he could not think of a word in the English (or any other) language to describe the action; and finally, upon consultation with Reverend Martinet, who favored the onomatopoeic "poot," and Doctor Nattering, who declared that "splught" would serve, he resolved the issue by spilling cappuccino on the page, obscuring the entire episode from record.

height of her roll he laid on the first stroke. "Oh that deedly doodly stings," cried Flanders, enormously loud.

The men tittered. Captain Audibly glared at them ferociously, holding his hand to his mouth to cover his own titter. Flanders was not a popular man on the ship, being openly religious and god-fearing by nature. He cried out at every stroke, variations on his opening theme, and mewled and whined like a girl when it was over. He always spoke in deedleys and diddley-iddleys; despite his religious natterings, Flanders had never learned to curse like a Christian.[11]

The day's fun over, the men returned to their work, holystoning and cleaning the deck of its rushet of gore, waiting for the sun to reach zenith, for the captain, with his omnipotence, to make it noon, for him to wind his chelengk and pipe them to dinner.

Captain Audibly enjoyed the company of some of his officers at dinner. Conversation was generally poor, as the men were, by tradition, not permitted to speak unless spoken to by the Captain, and he was usually too busy stuffing his face to speak to them. He did enjoy the poetry of Mr. Rowan and Mr. Martin, and generally had at least one of them to dinner every afternoon - usually both, as their poetical jealousy was a source of entertainment to him as much as the poetry itself. He had been aware of an unofficial competition going on between them for lo! these many voyages, each striving to create a greater sheer volume of words, with quality a distant second consideration; yet, both were of talent, and Captain Audibly enjoyed good poetry nearly as much as good music, although not nearly as much as good (or mediocre) food, or a good (or mediocre) woman.

This afternoon had been especially pleasant. The weather was pleasant, breezy enough to lay on a full spread of canvas, yet

---

[11] Historical note: In all likelihood, the reason for Captain Audibly's possibly over-harsh reaction to the foodfight stems from his awareness that the 1797 mutiny at Spithead had begun with a seemingly innocuous pillowfight that began aboard the *Erica* (26 1/2) and rapidly spread throughout the fleet, goosefeathers and eiderdown in such a flurry as to blot out the sun over a half-mile radius of the fleet's locus.

temperate for the time of year. Captain Audibly had passed some pleasant hours in the crosstrees, knitting Stephen a sweater of a becoming shade of green, to replace the one an inebriated sloth had thrown up on. Although he would have preferred a soft shade of maroon, the word had taken on unpleasant connotations to his nautical mind. Stephen, meanwhile, had been leaning over the side of a jollyboat, gazing at the sight of one-two-three-four-five, - six-seven-eight-nine-ten! Ten tiny turtles! Vogel, the bosun's mate, observing the doctor's attention, had gleefully netted them for soup.

Jack and Stephen sauntered into the galley to check on the dinner preparations (and to nibble out of the pot). Quillick was peeling potatoes. Jack picked one up from the pan. It was fair-sized, firm and unpeeled. He closed his hand upon it, squeezed, and the potato squirted out between his fingers in mushy streams. The pulpy remnant he dropped back into the pan and turned away. Stephen cackled, a nautical phrase coming unbidden to his mind.

"It looks as though you had caught a Tater," he croaked.

At dinner, Jack seated Dr. Nattering at his immediate right, as usual; Stephen had a fairly poor appetite, and rarely objected aloud to Jack's spearing a particularly succulent tidbit off his plate. Jack noted that Nattering had a fragment of pepperoni stuck in his wig, but said nothing. Mr. London, the sailmaker, sat on the Captain's left, a consolation for the sullying of his canvases, and his friend, Mr. Mjollnir, next to him. Mr. Rowan and Mr. Martin sat opposite each other along the sides of the plank, Mr. Keating, the midshipman, was invited as a comfort to Mr. Mjollnir, to please Mr. London, although not seated near Mjollnir; Jack having been perturbed at a previous dinner, when Mr. Keating had twitched and squirmed throughout five removes. Mr. Northington, the captain of the marines sat opposite Mr. Keating, for the purpose of kicking his shins right sharply should he misbehave; Mr. Mowell rounding it out, and Tom Pushings sat at the far end of the table.

They ate steadily, punctuated by occasional borborygmi and less occasional conversation. The captain started to discuss general naval tactics, until Dr. Nattering began to cackle. "Pardon me," he wheezed, "but to my knowledge, naval tactics is an oxymoron; the only naval tactics I've ever heard are limited to 'just run right at them.'"

"Did the doctor call the captain a moron?" Northington asked Rowan.

"It's a literary word," Rowan explained. "It's something that contradicts itself, like 'Epicurean pessimism,' or 'happy seaman.'"

"Indeed," Nattering added. "Like 'good morning,' or the single-worded oxymoron, 'monosyllabic.'" He continued to cackle. "Naval tactics! Indeed, it is limited to 'He who hesitates is crossed!'"

Jack sighed with contentment as he sucked quietly on a cow shank. This was so much better than his last voyage, when they had early finished off all the cattle and were reduced to eating boiled tuna-fish (the roast beef of old Calcutta), boiled codfish (the roast beef of old Rome), and boiled salted horse (the roast beef of old Dublin) - much to the regret of Mr. Jagiello, whose horse it had been.

Stephen, uncharacteristically, contributed to the flow of genial conversation, separating out the weevils from his biscuits and describing them to the company—the *tenebrios,* the *ptinus*, and the *phalangium cancroides*, and how to distinguish them for future reference, and what to look for in weevils in general.

When the brandy was poured, and Mr. Keating had fallen asleep consequently thereof, Captain Audibly asked Rowan and Martin if they should care to recite.

"With all my heart," responded the one; and "If it pleases you," echoed the other.

With a purse of two weevily biscuits as the prize for the better verse, and the assembled company as panel (save the Captain, who professed neutrality, and Mr. Keating, who was trembling in his sleep as from a bad dream), they took turns in recitation; Mr. Rowan proceeding first, as Mr. Martin had done the previous dinner. Rowan sipped his brandy, cleared his throat, and began:

Old longings nomadic leap,
Chafing at custom's chain;
Again from its brumal sleep
Wakens the ferine strain.

"That's capital," Mr. London burst out. "May I hear it again?"
He made quick notes in his pocketbook, and seemed inordinately
pleased by the ditty.

"Very fine, indeed," murmured the assemblage. "Excellent
vocabulary, meter, and imagery."

Then it was Mr. Martin's turn. He had not thought as much of
Rowan's work as the others seemed to do; it sounded to his ear
futuristically anachronistic. He asked Dr. Nattering if he
recognized the style.

"I am afraid not," replied Stephen. "It cannot be an ancient,
however."

Martin took a sip of his own brandy, and stood on his chair to
recite:

The Coming Snow

Aimless wind
Talking to lonely sky
Formless and void in the night above
No longer steel-arched and high
You huddle closer to Earth's tired frown
For warmth
And shiver frost from your cloak
The first flakes come sighing softly down.

"Very fine, indeed," murmured the assemblage. "Excellent
vocabulary, meter, and imagery."

To the annoyance of the participants, the contest was adjudged
a tie; each co-victor was required to eat a biscuit.

The cloth was drawn, the almonds eaten, the brandy drunk for a while, then dribbled, and finally spilled; the Captain thanked the diners for their excellent company, and they withdrew, nodding their thanks for the excellent food and the excellent entertainment.

Jack Audibly strolled out on his quarterdeck, replete. The evening salt spray revived his soul and spirits. Blessedly unlike his canvas, the days were shortening, and Polaris could already be seen to wink at him, as *Aghast* pressed onward toward the American side of the puddle. The pepperoni stains in the sails could hardly be seen in the gloaming *demi-jour*.

10

Another day ensued, as one might have expected. Jack was at the lee-rail, committing his first breakfast to the sea with gratifyingly accustomed ease to make room for the second. Stephen was spending considerable time in the crosstrees, scanning for seabirds with his glass. Jack joined him in a while, munching something nondescript which he did not offer to share. They fell to talking, in the casual way of old friends, neither pausing to hear out the other before continuing with his own thoughts. Jack tried, in his usual fashion, to educate Stephen in the ways of the mariner.

"You were no doubt curious about 'chappelling,'" he began. "I'm surprised you haven't asked me about it yet, as it is a most integral part of the operation of the ship, and every ship's boy and cat learns it, to be sure." Stephen cocked his head, attentively. Jack, heartened, continued. "Chappelling is called for when, instead of coming to, you are taken aback in light winds. You must put the helm up, if she has headway, haul up the mainsail and spinnaker, and square the after yards. Shift the helm as she gathers sternway, and when the after sails fill, and she gathers headway, shift your helm again. When she brings the wind aft, brace up the after yards, get the main tack down and sheet aft, and haul out the spinnaker as soon as it will take." Stephen continued to cock his head, but somewhat less attentively. His mind began to drift, and he considered purging Captain Audibly again. At such times, Stephen was grateful that he had two ears, so Jack's words could go in one and out the other.

"Fish in the water!" Stephen cried, but Jack considered the source of the cry, and continued placidly.

"Touch not the braces; the yards remain braced as before. We used to wear instead, by squaring the headyards when the after sails are full. This certainly had its advantages over chappelling, as the vessel will go off faster when the wind is abeam and abaft, and will come quicker when the wind gets on the other side, but chappelling..." Jack became aware that Stephen was talking to him.

"Linnaeus had carried on with Aristotle's notion of classifying all the animal kingdom into two groups," Stephen was explaining for the hundredth time. "Aristotle called them *enaima* and *anaima*, or animals with blood and animals without blood. You understand, of course, that by the word 'blood' he designated only the red fluid circulating in the higher animals; whereas you surely ken that a fluid somewhat akin to blood circulates in all the animals, albeit variously coloured, and even colourless in some..."

Stephen looked at Jack, who did not seem to be taking in a word, as usual. As Jack paused in his discussion of chappelling, Stephen continued, but in Latin. "To species and genera, however, Linnaeus, that great man, added orders, and classes, for example, dividing the animal kingdom into six classes: mammalia, aves, herpetons, pisces, insectivora, and annelids ..."

"I don't think the old fart understood a word I said," Jack complained, to no-one in particular.

"*D'anam d'an dial*," Stephen replied, to no-one in particular.

"*Du zelst vochsen vee ah tsibila mitten kup in drehrt*," responded Jack, to no-one in particular.

Stephen's yellow eyes narrowed. "HoD pIn'a' DenIb Qatlh of a veQDuj," he exclaimed, in a tone that was harsh even for Klingonese.

Jack shrugged his huge shoulders, mystified but grinning, and made the sign of the doubled vee "live long" with both hands.

"Which they're always going on about 'confusion to Boney,'" Quillick whispered to Baretta Blondin. "And all it would take would be for him to stand with his ears between those two."

Stephen Nattering usually slept in on Sunday mornings; this morning, however, he was awakened by a heated discussion, seemingly right beside his ear outside his cabin. He turned over, but the voices penetrated the thin wood. It was Mr. Adroa, Mr. Hai-

Uri, Mr. Tyr, and Mr. Paul Efimus, arguing loudly over who amongst them was the most devoted admirer of Admiral Nelson; who most like him in every thought and deed and aspect. Sighing, Stephen arose, dusted his face, and shuffled out of the cabin.

Captaincy was a lonely occupation, Jack thought. Stephen was the only one on board he could really talk to about his problems, fears, lusts, hopes, private thoughts, and occasional self-doubts. Stephen was again with him in the cross-trees, a fairly safe place to talk, since they could, from here, see Quillick or any other quidnunc who attempted to eavesdrop. "Eavesdrop," Stephen mused. "An odd choice of words to be used on a ship, don't you agree?" Jack agreed. Stephen was unusually pleasant this day, undoubtedly having indulged himself in opiate tincture recently, or the leaves of the coca which he now favored, when available.

"I don't much care for Mr. Mjollnir, the Dutch-built slab-sided bugger." Jack began. "He drinks too much; such men are dangerous."

"Faith, *plures crapula quam gladius*," replied Stephen.

"I do most sincerely regret that scrub Picard taking my carpenter," Jack continued. "I have little use for a bald-headed captain, I must say. May his bowels gush out. May his veins collapse."

"Sure, Jack," Stephen mollified him. "May God plant a *Ferocactus wislizenii* cactus on his head. But it's gone and done, so make what you can of it. *Non illegitimi te Carborundum*, we Papists say. And it's not like you to bear a grudge as you do against Picard. Have ye not heard the aphorism, sometimes attributed to that noble savage, the American Indian, 'don't criticize a man until you have walked a mile in his shoes?'"

Jack considered the matter slowly, as he considered most matters. "That's a capital idea," he exclaimed. "That way, when you criticize him, you'll be a mile away, and you'll have his shoes, too. Then the shoe will be..."

"On the other hand?" Stephen asked.

"Just so," Jack smiled. His smile turned downward. "Just so, I suppose."

It was nippy in the crosstops. Jack pulled down the flaps of his astrakhan hat and hugged himself. "I know Nelson never needed a coat—love of England kept him warm, but I'm shivering," he muttered.

Stephen studied him thoughtfully. "That's not exactly the way it happened," he ventured. "I have it directly from Dr. Thomas Blagrave himself that there is more to that story than what is commonly bruited."

Jack perked his ears, always keen for Nelsoniana.

"Nelson rarely wore a coat," Stephen said slowly, "because he was frequently burning with malaria. The 'love of England' bit was something he tossed out to inspire the troops, and to downplay his illness."

With a profound sigh of relief, Jack smiled affectionately at his friend, gratefully buttoning his teal-blue velvet-collared wraprascal.

A rather strange event occurred early in the cruise. One of the younger midshipmen, Mr. Momos, was unusually rowdy, even for a boy. He was roaring away in the tops, following a wet-towel fight amongst the young gentlemen. "Pipe down, Mr. Momos," yelled Captain Audibly in exasperation, boxing Momos' ears like a compass. To his horror, his cry was instantly relayed, and "Pipe down" echoed through the ship, picked up by the bosun, who promptly sounded the pipe. Throughout the ship, men left their posts, unrelieved, and raced to their hammocks. Audibly couldn't be angry with them; it was a sign of their instant obedience to orders, which ought to have been encouraged; yet, the ship luffed badly, and it was some time before order was restored.

"The smudge of seaweed just above the cathead is of an odd color, is it not?" Jack asked Stephen, one particularly pleasant day.

"That projecting piece of wood just below the *alga marina* is the cathead, is it?" Stephen replied. "You'll have noticed, I'm sure, the lack of stamens or pistils on the alga, signifying that there can be no true flowers to it. Did you say 'cathead?'"

Jack nodded his head, unwilling to comment on Stephen's long-standing curiosity about the names for the parts of the ship, and his equally long-standing refusal to retain any of the terms asked about - this was perhaps the fifth time this voyage that the cathead had been identified.

"My dear, shall I tell you why it is called the 'cathead?'" Stephen continued smoothly.

Jack shuddered involuntarily. He was certain that this discussion would lead to no good—it would no doubt lead to a description of a proposed modification to the structure of the bow of the ship for the benefit of the Royal Navy, such as suspending a horizontal plank appending to the cathead so that a natural philosopher could sit on it and dangle his feet while perusing the sea for odd life-forms.

Stephen waited, frowning. Jack's inherent amiability and good will rose despite himself. "By all means; nothing would please me more," he smiled. "I've never been certain in my own mind as to the nautical terminology, and would welcome enlightenment; I should like it of all things. Why indeed is that 'projecting piece of wood' termed 'cathead?'"

Stephen cackled dryly. "Because the anchor is <u>mewed up</u> against it while the ship is <u>feelin'</u> its way out of the harbour!"

Jack scratched his chin dubiously, but then began to roar with laughter as the meaning of Stephen's words sunk in. His bright blue eyes sparkled and watered, his bellies jiggled, his laughter ripped through the ship, and every man aboard, awake and asleep, smiled happily at the sound of it.

Captain Audibly continued to favor the boy, Keating, who was blossoming under the attention and tutelage. He had learned the constellations of the night sky, and was mastering his takings of longitudes and latitudes, although he sometimes came up with very wild reckonings. Jack noted with concern the boy's posture— hunched over defensively; he always seemed coiled, tensed as if to dart away at the sign of corporal punishment or sexual affront, yet too paralyzed by abject terror to run at any given moment. It offended Jack that the boy should fear him so—he acknowledged the general fear that a captain strikes in the men under his omnipotent command, and encouraged it as a means of discipline, *ira principis mort est*; yet he had given this boy no particular reason for such unholy dread. The lad was no coward in some other regards Jack had noticed—although the youngest of the midshipmen's berth, he attempted to hold his own in boxing matches the boys staged against each other, and he did not allow the bigger boys to bully him out of his meagre rations. He showed occasional bruises about his face, arms and legs, although that was commonplace enough at sea to warrant no attention at all, except that Jack knew him to be graceful for his age, despite the increasing coltishness of his limbs. He oft-times limped around the deck, walking crookedly even for a seaman. Yet, when questioned about his stiffnesses, he denied any awareness of pain or soreness. If the older boys were beating him out of jealousy for his being Mr. Mjollnir's special catamite, Jack had heard nothing of it.

Keating seemed reluctant to climb the rigging, too. He did so when asked, unquestioningly, but from below, glanced upwards more often than was necessary; and from above, glanced downwards even more timorously. Jack thought that practice would cure him of acrophobia, if that was the problem. "I'm going up to the topgallantyard masthead," he told the youth; "pray bring me my glass." He hung back at the crosstrees, watching Keating inch his way up, far too slowly. To speed the boy's progress, he flicked a sharp lash at him with a bight of rope. Keating froze, panicky, looked at the captain, and seemed to open his hands in despair. He plummeted from the rigging, landing hard on his right side. Jack slid down with extraordinary speed for a man of his size. He could see Keating's shattered bones protruding from his arm.

Keating's eyes were wide, unseeing. "Say, father, say, if yet my task be done," he whispered.

Jack summoned Dr. Nattering, who came with unusual alacrity; one look told him that the arm would have to come off - it was too far damaged to set. He had worked miracles at times, as when he brought young Mr. Harper back from the dead, but the arm was beyond repair.

Jack deeply regretted the incident. The younker would be of no further use to any navy ship, of course. He would have to be invalided back to England on the next homeward bound vessel they encountered. "Now, now," he comforted Mr. Keating. "It's not so bad as you think. You can always be a ratcatcher, a dustman, a fishmonger, a swineherd, or a civil servant."

"Or a chimneysweep," Dr. Nattering added as he finished sealing and cauterizing the stump by dipping it in hot pitch. He finished by administering a powerful cathartic to the boy. It would temporarily take his mind off whatever else had happened to him. Stephen had found that this worked particularly effectively with his dental patients as well. In his experience, men who visited the doctor were pleased to see tangible results of their treatment, and a clysma or aperient was a most positive palliative for almost all ailments to be found on shipboard.

"Don't take it hard, now," Jack continued. "It's not the end of the world." He turned to Dr. Nattering. "Would ye care to join me for some toasted cheese?"

They took their snack in the Captain's dining cabin. Jack asked Stephen, "Pray, pass me the small package from the shelf to starboard." Stephen scanned diligently to larboard, not finding it. Jack glanced at him.

"I wonder," he noted, "That a person with your ear for languages should have so much difficulty in distinguishing 'starboard' from 'larboard.'"

Stephen brindled. "Sure, and I know the one from t'other. But the trouble is when the ship is facing in the opposite direction." Jack considered on this for a while, his genial countenance slowly clouding over.

A similar incident occurred some days later. They were passing some snow-tipped islands at a distance. In the crosstrees, Jack attempted to attract Stephen's attention to a bird he saw in the leeward distance. Stephen lifted his glass and peered to windward. "Stephen," said Jack, not at all unkindly. "I said 'leeward.' You really need to improve your listening skills."

"Not at all, not at all, my dear," replied Stephen. "I don't have your omnipotent powers to raise the sun and make it noon. Nor can I possibly improve on the glistening hills." Jack averted his eyes, and slid down to the deck.

The snake Stephen had snuck aboard was not working out well. Stephen had hoped that the snake would eat the ship's rats, which he believed to be responsible for disease on some vessels; unhappily, it only ate one rat per week, not nearly enough to accomplish anything, although several of the hands had cheered when it ate a certain gerbil, studded pink leathern collar and all. Worse, it had a tendency to coil itself around the rigging, startling the men who grabbed handholds of rope whenever climbing, and found it inconvenient when a presumed rope was unattached to anything substantial, and slithered away just as they shifted their weight onto it. The issue was resolved on dark night, when the midshipmen caught it and ate it—it tasted like raw chicken, but they had eaten far worse.

For a time, Stephen blamed Jack for the disappearance of his snake, but had no proof of malfeasance. He had known mariners to be aelurophobic (as was Napoleon Buonaparte), but couldn't understand why his friend so disliked every wee beastie Stephen had ever introduced. Jack had once gone so far as to use a patently false explanation of the origin of the term "horse latitudes" as his excuse for coldly executing an entire colony of wasps Stephen had been studying for weeks; just as he was about to learn and write up the mysteries of wasp reproduction abnormalities caused by nervous stress. Eventually, under questioning, one of the mids admitted that he had seen the snake to wash overboard, but hadn't said anything for fear of upsetting the doctor. Although aware that he had unjustly maligned his dear friend, Stephen's conscience pricked him not at all, in his certain knowledge that Jack had disposed of many of his pets by violence or cookery.

Stephen dreamed one night of an onrushing tidal wave—the roar was deafening. He jerked awake, but still heard the roar—it was Jack Audibly, snoring, inches from his ear. He stumbled still half-enveloped in his dream onto the deck during a squall, and was riveted by a thoroughly unusual movement in the choppy sea. His entire conscious attention was now wholly taken up with the most striking, moving, and unexpected sight he had ever seen. As his eyes followed a pod of bottlenose dolphins swimming rapidly westwards in the glassy wall rearing before him, they met a vast shape swimming east. He instantly knew that it couldn't be what it appeared, it must be, but it was impossible; but for a moment, his mind was so astonished, amazed that he cried out "Mrs. Williams' derriere! Mrs. Williams' derriere!" but Baretta Blondin rushed to his side reassuringly; it was merely a whale.

"I'm sure I wasn't snoring," Jack muttered groggily when Stephen returned.

"Tell that to the remaining stars," Stephen sighed.

They passed a convoy of homeward ships. Signals flew; Mr. Keating was transferred with honours in the captain's own gig. Stephen looked at him sadly. "Sure, and I'm not the renifleur like Mr. Blabbington, but the boy always has the smell of pistachio nuts about his curved neck," he said.

"A most admirable little chap," Jack replied. "I do hope he finds employment back home. He showed promise, I'd hoped to share with him my true enthusiasm for the sea..."

He stopped in mid-sentence. After the official signals had been displayed, the signalmen of the various ships had continued communicating, as was the usual course of events. News and gossip traveled rapidly in the Royal Navy. Jack was dismayed to catch a glimpse of the "foodfight" flag being lowered from the mast of the ship nearest his and hoisted on the next - he had dared hope that the disgraceful incident had ended with the floggings.

Stephen noticed his dismay. "It seems odd," he remarked, "that the French have never learned to read our signals, after all these years we've been at odds with them. I suspect the cause is genetic: they killed off all the intellectuals during the Red Terror beginning in 1789; the current generation is much stupider; partly genetic, I suppose, and perhaps partly due to the interruption of the lines of culture and thought." It lead Jack to wonder why Stephen had never learned to read the signals, after all his years at sea, but he prudently held his tongue, not wanting to be bled again. He thought over Stephen's words. Stephen was an intellectual, and his abstract thoughts were oft-times of great value; but Jack's strength was his practical experience of the world of war—he believed the reason for the French inability to decipher flags was their inexperience at it—they had not had enough man-hours at sea to have seen enough British signals to build a base for deciphering. He turned to Stephen for discussion, but he was already lost in study of a seabird, and not to be disturbed.

Yet, Stephen was usually an excellent listener. In fact, Jack Audibly was, too. It was one of the mainstays of their long friendship that they could talk to each other for hours on end, day after day after day, year after year, and neither had heard everything the other thought, because their thoughts continued to evolve. Stephen pondered on this facet of their relationship to each other, even as he studied his precious birds. "Sure, and it's a manifestation of the grand 'Principle of Description' we hear so much about," he thought. "As you describe something, you become more aware of it. The more you describe something, the more you discover and understand about it." And Stephen and Jack had described so many of their thoughts and perceptions to each other, they had both grown immeasurably over the years as a direct result of the relationship. "It must surely be the first law of psychology," Stephen continued to ponder. "You get more of what you reinforce." By not squelching Audibly's technobabble discussions of seamanship, but by listening to him, as patiently as he could, given the subject, he had added immeasurably to

Audibly's love of and understanding of nautical matters. It didn't matter if Stephen neither understood nor cared about the subject—his attention had reinforced Jack's description and deep, even subconscious understandings. And Jack Audibly had done much the same for Stephen's love of natural history, again without ever understanding the subject or learning anything from Stephen's descriptions of birds and sloths and lice. He was certain that Audibly understood the Principle of Description, although they had never discussed it; he was well aware that Audibly insisted on all his midshipmen keeping a journal, not only of naval matters, but of their thoughts and views on the sights they observed in their travels. Such a journal would provide a reinforcement of observations, thus rendering the writer more sensitive to his surroundings and reinforcing the very act of observation and attentiveness to one's observations. You get more of what you reinforce. If you reward yourself for noticing things, you will notice more, and understand more. Stephen smiled, and the smile turned his thoughts to humour.

"Can you tell me," he asked Jack, his sallow lips spread into what passed for a grin, "what's the difference between bentinck shrouds and an elephant expecting a calf?"

Jack stared at him. Stephen was definitely smiling. Jack started grinning too, in anticipation of a great *bon mot* he could pass on as his own at the next gunroom dinner. "Tell me, pray," he said, chuckling eagerly.

Stephen merely looked at him, feigning sadness. "Sure, and I thought you would know, but don't fret your head, for all love," Stephen reassured him. "I'll ask Tom Pushings. I'm sure he'll know."

He chuckled dryly as they turned into Jack's cabin for their nightly music.

"Are we to play the andante from the Locatelli thirty-seventh sonata again?" Stephen asked with mild irritation.

"Is there some reason not to? I think it's rather pretty, myself, and it keeps Sophie in my mind. She plays it prodigious well on the piano, you know."

"Pretty it is, the first few times, perhaps," Stephen replied, sawing the air with his bow for emphasis. "But to my mind, the idea of a duet is that we both play, and the role of the 'cello in this piece is a mere pla-plink-plunk, pla-plink-plunk, right on forever, with never a port de voix, fioritura, trilleto, bebung, appoggiatura, pralltriller, acciaccatura, or even a double mordent!"

Jack smirked. "Now we're getting to the nux of the matter. Do you like that word, by the by? It's for nub, crux, and nexus, all rolled into one! But as to the piece - you want to be lead virtuoso all the time, and this segment lets the violin carry the tune for a while."

"Carry it?" Stephen wondered. "Carry it where?"

"Besides," Jack interrupted. "The 'cello has more to do than you credit, if only you didn't rush the matter, and if you played it

with proper affection, and not so loudly... and with a gentle reflective elegance..."

Stephen picked up his 'cello and bow with an air of deep resignation. He would not for the world deprive Jack of this relief from the cares and weight of his office.

Suddenly there came an interruption. "Sail ho! Sail ho!" Stephen felt the breeze as Audibly raced past, and indeed, it seemed, a jerk in the nearly six hundred ton ship, as Jack Audibly raced up to the maintop.

"Sails ho!" came the cry again. "Two sails, and another."

Stephen peered out, but saw nothing but sea and sky. "They ain't ours, neither. They're stars and stripes, and they're turning toward us. They see us! They see us! They're turning this way."

A cloud seemed to form over the *Aghast,* but unluckily, it was only a darkening of the collective mood of the ship, because broad daylight stretched ahead, way too many hours of it.

11

"Bend on all the sail she'll bear!" roared Captain Audibly from the top. The topsmen were already at the braces, and sheeted her home with alacrity. The sails billowed, and the ship began to heel. "Let's get the _____ out of here!" Jack roared, sliding down the backstay. They turned and fled, packing on sail after sail. Jack put his glass, a Dullard anachronistic, on the Americans. They were already hull up, and gaining, but the stiff west southwesterly wind filled the *Aghast*'s sails, and she was capable of making great speed when properly handled; and Captain Audibly's crew was well practiced as well as well-motivated. The lead American ship, a thirty-two-gun frigate, was gaining on them; it was perhaps seven miles away and carrying well; the two larger ships-of-the-line were falling behind but carrying full sail and wouldn't be behind by far. Yet, watching with narrowed eyes and pursed lips, Audibly thought they could outrun the Americans with a bit of luck. "A great bit of luck," he thought, but perhaps it could be done.

"A boat," said Stephen, as he dropped down onto the deck, turning to go below to his station in the sick-berth.

"Clap onto the doctor," Captain Audibly roared out, but it was too late. The ship heaved, and although Baretta Blondin swooped out and grazed the doctor's outstretched fingertips, Stephen flung overboard, his wig flying incongruously into the sea, followed by the splash of the doctor. Instantly, the men began hurling, anything that came to hand, in hopes that the doctor could grasp something to keep afloat until rescue. Pizzas sailed over his head in great profusion; he ducked gracelessly to avoid thrown marlin spikes; chicken coops with squawking chickens and geese landed all around him and instantly sank; small deckboys were thrown to his rescue, most of them unable themselves to swim, adding to the general melee; Mr. Readey threw biscuits methodically, one after another; a small anchor fell a few inches short of his skull, and he gagged convulsively on the splash; one grizzled sailor took advantage of the situation to heave Stephen's collection of Norwegian rats overboard in the doctor's general direction. The ocean suddenly teemed with feathers and fur and paraphernalia, Stephen Nattering gamely dodging it all, flailing wildly to fend off the drowning poultry.

"Helm alee!" roared Audibly, leaping to the rail. He glanced at the American frigate. "We are captured," he cried, as he leaped into the ocean.

The way came off the *Aghast* as she turned into the wind. He swam out, and grabbed Stephen's frail body with his massive forearm, striking back toward the ship. *Aghast*'s marines were already lining the rail, guns at the ready, watching for sharks; sailors also lined the rail, tossing lines over toward their beloved captain and equally beloved doctor. There was not a man aboard who did not believe he owed his very life to one or the other, and mostly, to both. Jack tied Stephen to a line, and watched him hauled aboard even as he himself clapped onto another line and hoisted himself up.

The pursuit by the Americans was out of mind when the doctor and the captain were on the deck. Eager hands reached out to rub them down, to strip them of their wet clothes and wrap them in dry, to rub their hair dry, to proffer hot coffee, blankets, whatever they could reach.

Stephen looked over the side of the ship, longingly, as his wig floated away. He shot an imploring glance at Jack, but didn't press the issue.

The doctor was led below, shivering violently. Jack turned his attention back to the American frigate, and was astonished to find her stopped in the water, no closer than she had been when first he had leaped, perhaps thirty minutes earlier.

On board the *Pueblo* (78), the antics of the British frigate had caused considerable consternation for the young American commodore.

"They've turned!" he shouted to the captain and his lieutenants unnecessarily, as they, too, had their glasses on the chase. "'Hoy, lookouts!" he bellowed up. "What do you see?"

"They've turned," cried down the lookouts, their shrill pipes being relayed down along the line.

"What do you see beyond?" shouted up Commodore Bucher.

The lookouts strained, but saw nothing.

Commodore Bucher thought hard. He knew, both from training and from his limited experience, that the Royal Navy had very limited guile in their naval maneuvers. They lived and breathed by Admiral Nelson's exhortation, "Never mind the tactics—just run right at them." But they wouldn't run right at two ships-of-the-line and a thirty-two-gun frigate with their twenty-eight-gun frigate—it just didn't make sense. It didn't make sense at all. Why had they turned?

Had they seen reinforcements on their horizon, out of sight of his own, nine or ten miles further east? Were they the vanguard of a British invasionary fleet? This had been long-expected, of course. It was just a matter of time before the British came—they'd sent numerous ships over since the commencement of the hostilities, and several expeditionary forces—was this the main invasion? Bucher thought as hard as he could, scratching his head beneath his commodore's cap.

"What do you see now?" he asked up the masthead, but again, they saw nothing. He signaled to the *Touchnought*, under Ness, but they saw nothing either.

"Still," he thought, "they've fallen off, so they'll likely be turning, coming after us with a whole goddammed fleet. I'll not risk our two warships and the frigate just to grab off a goddammed little frigate of theirs, even if she seems to be a sweet sailor on a bow-line." Reluctantly, very reluctantly, he sent signal to the *Touchnought* and his frigate to put their own helms alee, and watch to see if more English appeared.

Audibly, meanwhile, was puzzled. Why hadn't the Americans taken the *Aghast* when they had the chance? They should have been boarded by now—instead, the frigate was still seven miles off, and the men-of-war even further, and stopped. He thought. He thought some more.

He remembered a somewhat similar incident that had occurred on *La Minerve*. "Could it be?" he wondered.

"Set a kedge," he whispered to Mr. Aeolos, the master. Looking askance, Aeolos had a kedge dropped quietly over the side. To the Americans, it would look like he had reversed course and was beating westward, towards them, but he would progress no nearer to them. As soon as it became apparent that he had reversed himself, and was sailing towards the Americans, a new signal hoisted above the *Pueblo*, and the Americans reversed course and hightailed it away.

"I'll be damned," crowed Audibly exuberantly.

"Probably," whispered Aeolos under his breath, but aloud he said nothing at all. All hands began to cheer, but Captain Audibly cut them off with a booming "Silence fore and aft!" The situation was still grave. They watched for a while, the masts seemingly straining under the winds, trying to beat back westward, but stilled by the kedge. When it was evident that the danger was past, Audibly allowed a mighty cheer to raise, as they pulled the kedge and raced eastward to obscurity and safety. Audibly sanctioned a bonus rum ration to the men, and they got rousingly, satisfyingly drunk. There was cheering and strutting and chicken noises from the maindeck, and Rowan summed the feelings of the Royal Navy towards the poltroon American rebels quite well: "We have not yet begun to fight," he paraphrased, "and we're not going to, neither." Captain Audibly was as pleased by the citation as he had been by anything he had ever heard from Rowan.

Jack went below to the sick-berth, where Stephen was still shivering. He embraced his dear friend, and they had steaming hot portable soup together. Their friendship had endured for nearly two decades; despite a difference of nearly fifteen years in their ages, despite their profound differences in temperament, appetites, radically different interests, different approaches to life, differences in nearly everything one would think should matter—what they had in common (apart from carnal knowledge of Diana) was curiosity, interest in life itself, love of music, love of ideas, and the interchange of thoughts. Their relationship had been like a dance— sometimes a minuet, sometimes a scherzo, sometimes a tango, sometimes a tumble of arms and legs—but they had sensed each other's souls from the start, and like wild geese, had pair-bonded forever.

"Ye'd have given up the ship for me, *cushlamochree?*" Stephen asked, incredulously.

"A hundred times over," Jack said, his eyes misting.

Stephen, too, was misty-eyed. Jack was touched at his friend's gratitude. He thought back to the dozens of men he had rescued from the sea. It always astounded him that men would be unable to swim, even when their lives depended on it. It astounded him even more when they were not only ungrateful for his rescue, but downright hostile, as if they soon would have sprouted water wings, or learned to walk upon the water, had he not interfered. He remembered the pearl diver he had plucked from the China Sea; the cliffdiver off Acapulco; neither had been grateful at all when Audibly, upon seeing them hit the water, had halted his own ship and leaped to their rescue. "Damned ungrateful, as much so as American Indians had been for their civilization," he thought to himself again. Quillick came below, and rebraided Jack's long, streaming hair while they enjoyed their soup, and gradually, warmth and life returned to their extremities.

Captain Audibly stood in the maintop, scanning the horizons, The Americans were nowhere to be seen, nor were there any other ships in sight. He rejoiced in the error he realized the Americans had made, rejoiced in his freedom, now so much dearer to him for its having been threatened, rejoiced in his friend's safety, rejoiced at life itself! The moon rose, red-wreathed and joyous, seemingly smiling, as if in response to Jack's rising exuberance.

12

They took two merchantmen during the next two days; *Arcturus*, seventeen-hundred-ton burden, and *Orion*, fifteen-hundred - American-built ships, carrying American cargoes. One stood fairly intact; they had been forced to hole the second so severely that she poured water to an extent reminiscent of Cedargrove Cottage. They inventoried the supplies and stores and cargoes of their prizes, and found new-modeled American rifles, fowling guns, pistols, tobacco, pine tar, bourbon, rum, raccoon fur caps with the tails still attached, several copies of the Colonies' Declaration of Independence (the historical value of which had been destroyed, however, by marginal scribblings by the authors), cranberries ("that grateful polychrestic antiscorbutic!") exulted Stephen, who promptly added it to the men's rations, supplementing that day's oatmeal, cheese, and sushi; cotton, American money (always very welcome for local service needs, not booty), and excellent pine, fir for masts, elm for keels, and lovely, lovely thick oak wood - nearly twenty tons of lumber. How welcome that would be back in England, where whole forests had been decimated during the exhaustive war of the past two decades! Jack Audibly had marveled at the vast quantities of timber that had been required for the building of a single ship of the line; the *Victory*, for example, had exhausted sixty acres of forest to provide the two thousand oak trees needed for her construction, and England was fast running out of forests. They found American grain, bound for France. To Captain Audibly's mind, the French did not need grain - they still had dogs,[12] snails, frogs, and at the end of the war, wouldn't they learn to enjoy haggis, too, and bashed neeps (neeps hackit with balmagowry). Jack smiled a grim smile.

---

[12] Ed. note: Although natural selection was unknown at the time this saga took place, the evolution of miniature poodles was a direct adaptive result of wartime famines in France during the Napoleonic adventures.

The conclusion of war-time conditions would achieve more than just restoration of the monarchy and the way things should be—with renewed amity between the nations, England would in all likelihood be proud to send over a few cooks to teach the French how to properly boil their food. The grain would be more nobly diverted to feed John Bull. They helped themselves to all the powder they could find, the small arms, and a generous supply of the tobacco, bourbon and rum, as well as several barrels of the cranberries, which were deliciously tart. Officers and hands alike feasted that afternoon on fresh beef, fresh vegetables, fresh water, fresh soft bread, and cranberries. No-one had ever accused Captain Audibly of gross stupidity; he had the men's cranberries well mashed into a gruelly mush before releasing the supply.

Stephen Nattering was profoundly disturbed by what he considered an especially atrocious barbarity amid the usual barbarity of sea battle. He finally summoned up the courage to ask Captain Audibly about it. "It is bad enough that you shoot to kill or maim the humans on the other ship, but is it truly necessary to try to blind them too?" Jack was puzzled by the remark.

"I was not aware of any particular effort in that regard," he said somberly. "Pray tell me the details, and I will see to the disciplining of the officer involved."

"But, my love, it was you yourself I speak of. As we neared the enemy ship, I clearly and distinctly heard you to order the gunners to fire on their eyes."

Jack Audibly laughed until the tears streamed from his eyes, his massive stomach heaving with convulsions. "Pardon me, I beg your forgiveness," he chortled. "What I intended to say was for the gunners to fire on the rise!" Unmollified by the lame excuse, Stephen descended to the sick-berth to tend to the few injuries that had suffered during the battles, and to prepare a potent slime-draught for Captain Audibly.

Jack sent off Tom Pushings and a small prize crew in one of the ships, and lieutenant James Mowell in the other, begging each safe voyage and speedy return from Canada, because he was already short-handed. Although there had been no combat since they'd left

England, nearly a month earlier, the very sailing of a war frigate took its toll on the men. He'd had live cannon practice every night, as usual for Audibly; although that resulted in numbers of injuries, sprains, broken bones, abdominal ruptures, and burns, it was the only way to keep a fighting ship in tune; and well worth the cost, to Audibly's mind.

After gunnery practice one night, Stephen and Jack were making music.

"Damn your Proddy eyes!" Stephen roared of a sudden. "There you go again, Captain. If you're going to hum out of metre, the least you could do is to try to approximate the pitch or the key!"

Jack looked at him, hurt welling from his usually merry eyes. "I wasn't humming a'tall," he protested.

"I don't mind that you make rumbling noises in your throat when you read anything more intellectually challenging than the *Naval Chronicle*, but this music merits better treatment than your harsh solfeggio," Stephen expostulated. "Perhaps it's the repertoire that causes it. Perhaps if we strove towards a more classical balance instead of these lyrical, romantic pieces by unknowns... "

"I've heard of Sir Roger Bromide," Jack interrupted.

"I suspect that the man never wrote this. More likely, he got Handel to ghost it for him, so he could come it the cultured gentleman instead of a rich merchant cove."

"I'll try not to hum," Jack said softly. "At any rate, let's not take it out on the music. Shall we begin again at section D?"

"May worms eat your bone marrow, but there you go humming again," Stephen exclaimed in disgust.

They reached the coast of Florida, and put Stephen Nattering on shore, Farbanti the stroke oar personally carrying him into the gig, and then from the gig onto the shore, so that he would not catch his death of cold from wet feet. Florida was an inhospitable swamp, and every man aboard trembled at the sight of alligators in the vicinity where the doctor alit, but he assured them that he would be perfectly safe with any of God's creatures except man. He described for them the digestive juices of the crocodiles, which contain so much hydrochloric acid that they can dissolve swallowed iron spearheads, and speculated as to whether the alligators' juices were equally strong, and the men fell back in awe, certain (rightly so) that he intended to determine the issue at first hand. The men believed he was going ashore on a naturalist's holiday, and were morally outraged that the captain would so endanger their doctor for the frivolous pursuit, but none dared speak his mind. Jack did not enlighten the men: he believed firmly in the proverb that brandy is Latin for a goose. Stephen and Jack calculated that the doctor would need no more than two weeks to meet up with his Indian contacts and set into play the diversionary activities that would allow an assault on New Orleans by the British troops already en route; Jack agreed to wear on and off every night from the twelfth, for ten nights, to pick Stephen up when he returned from the Indians. Some of the men were as frightened of the Indians as they were of the alligators, having heard tales of mindless savagery, but Stephen rejected the offer of Clumsy Dravis to accompany him for the purpose of out-cannibalizing the cannibals—Stephen assuring him that those were the other Indians he was thinking of, the ones in Asia.

Hard as they watched, and with raised glass, too, they lost sight of Stephen almost instantly he stepped on shore. He melted into the mangrove swamp and vanished as into thin air. Men who marveled at the doctor's inability to walk and breathe at the same time on anything that floated were equally incredulous of his ability to do both and more on land.

They sailed north again, to take up their station off Maryland. They sighted occasional British ships, but no more American vessels were seen, until they had reached the Chesapeake Bay, when they saw, at a great distance, an eighteen-gunner, sailing very poorly indeed. They crept closer, slowly, maintaining distance until they could smoke why she was missing stays so badly, luffing, deck awash. As they neared, wondering why they were not spotted, Audibly was in the tops, peering hard through his glass.

"Why, they're just mere boys," he exclaimed.

Boys they were, and reefing and dropping the sails in shifts, shifting topmasts, setting and weighing anchors, climbing and descending the riggings, running guns out and in, and hoisting out boats; clearly a training vessel. The lookout was fast asleep in the top.

The American ship, *Academy*, suddenly raised them, heeling sharply around to head into the protected area of the Bay, but Audibly could see that they would not reach it in time. The *Academy* fired a cannon into the air, and guns began firing from the Calvert Cliffs, but nowhere near to the *Aghast*, now racing at ten knots towards the Americans. It was indeed a training vessel, with a minimal complement of officers and what looked like one hundred fifty youth, ranging in age from nine to fourteen, and apparently, no professional crew to speak of in terms of seamanship.

As soon as it became evident that the *Aghast* was headed towards them and would reach them before they could reach safety, the Americans struck her colors and hoisted the white flag of surrender.

Although the *Aghast*'s guns were fully run out, every man in his place, Audibly gave the "Hold your fire!" command. They boarded the *Academy* without argument, Captain Hornbearer surrendering his sword to Audibly with a rueful nod, but not a bow.

After determining that the captured vessel did not have any *Grey Poupon*, Audibly accepted the sword, bowed deeply, turned it in his hands, and returned it to the American.

"Jack Audibly!" cried Hornbearer when names were exchanged. "Why, I've heard of you!"

Jack beamed, modestly.

"Would you be the same Jack Audibly, I wonder... Are you that," he paused, choking back "the pirate of the seven seas," again paused delicately, "excuse me, are you that 'goddam fat clumsy lobscouse' what spilled beef stew down Admiral Nelson's britches, by any chance?"

Jack was pleased that his meeting with Nelson had been noted, but wished he could have been better remembered.

"Thank you for not hurting my boys," said Hornbearer. "This being only the second time they've actually been on the water as a group; although they've had classroom hours, they need quite a few days of hard sailing to shape up." He paused. "I implore you not to press them. They're young lads and eager, but not ready for the harsh life in the British Royal Navy, not a one of them."

Audibly mustered the boys on deck, sending a few of his hands below to ferret out those who would hide.

Clumsy Dravis came back on deck, working his jaws furiously, to the alarm of his shipmates. All the boys watched him, grinning. The boarding crew watched him too, from a safe distance. As usual, a foam of spittle flecked his jaws, running freely down to his neck. Suddenly, a large pink bubble emerged from his mouth, expanded, and popped violently, all over his face and hair. He spat a pink blob onto the deck. Audibly noted that the deck was speckled with similar pink blotches, one of which was sticking to the sole of his boot. The boy with him was fondling a piece of stiffened paper, on which was drawn the likeness of what appeared to be a cricketeer. Audibly glanced at the blobs. They were similar in texture to a substance Dr. Nattering had obtained from a Dyak headhunter, made from the inspissated juice of the Malay gutta-percha tree, or perhaps it was the caoutchouc from Stephen's Brazilian friends?

One of the boys snickered. Dravis started towards him, his meatcleaver raised, salivating profusely, but stopped when Baretta Blondin seized a boathook menacingly.

There was little of use in the ship's boypower, and Audibly declined to press the two lieutenants, taking only their parole.

"I'll not press the lads," he told Captain Hornbearer. "I'll need about fifteen of the largest to man the sloop up to Canada under my lieutenant Wallingford, but if they'll bend to decent, I'll warrant their safe passage back home after."

"That's decent in you," Captain Hornbearer replied. "I'd appreciate it if you'd leave my son here with me, so's his mama won't worry about him." Audibly readily assented, and a tall, gangly, blebby lad of thirteen stepped to Hornbearer's side with a shy sigh of relief, standing somewhat behind Captain Hornbearer. Audibly stared at him. The boy looked not all like his father. Embarrassed, he averted his eyes so as not to shame Captain Hornbearer, who merely shrugged, rubbing his forehead meaningfully.

"I'll be requiring your larger gig," Audibly said, not mentioning that his requirement stemmed from his own gig being irrevocably stained with mashed potatoes and gravy from the foodfight. "You may start releasing the boys in groups in the smaller gig. As soon as they're off, I'd be honoured to entertain you and your lieutenants to dinner, and you're free to leave, of course, at any time."

"Delighted," replied Captain Hornbearer. "And you and your officers are welcome to my wife's fine cooking tomorrow evening, if you'll remain in the area. We have a fine store laid in from our autumn harvest, and you're in goose country now—I don't doubt we'll have fine roast goose with goose liver stuffing and chestnut dressing, and I pride myself on my country apple wine, which I put up myself."

Dinner on board *Aghast* was at three, and Jack Audibly was ravenous at the smell of the roasting meat they had liberated from the merchantmen, and the thought of wild goose the next day.

"I'm sorry to say we don't have any hotdogs; I know you Americans are partial to them, but I hope you'll enjoy our fine English cuisine," he said as he introduced Captain Hornbearer and his lieutenants to Mr. Rowan, Mr. Mjollnir, Mr. London, and Mr. Martin. They had a splendid *olla podrida,*[13] which Jack assured his guests was Nelson's favourite soup. Quillick had personally soused a pig's head that day, and they had plenty of spam with spam gravy, lobscouse, a fine catch of same-day rockfish, thrice-boiled solid English vegetables, and a rousingly successful gallimaufry. The cranberries added a nice dash of color, although Captain Audibly was momentarily panicked by the outlandish notion that his guests might take it into their heads to... but no, that was ridiculous. Food was food, and it was savored by all. For dessert, they enjoyed a magnificent spotted dog, with a dish of bacon grease for dipping. Quillick served with uncharacteristic efficiency, nothing was spilled, and the last of Audibly's good wine and his best sillery topped all.

Captain Hornbearer asked Captain Audibly's opinion on the war, and listened attentively to his response.

"Oh, how I wish my particular friend, Dr. Nattering, were here to enjoy your company. He loves intelligent conversation," said Audibly. "I do hope you'll meet him in a few weeks. But tell, pray, your own opinion on the subject."

---

13 *Olla Podrida* a la Nelson

Take a chicken, first-rate (cut-up, deboned), and a ham of eighty ounces (battered, basted, and cut up), and after sauteing two onions (diced), two stalks of celery (diced), and six cloves of garlic (diced) in olive oil, keep throwing in the chicken and ham, and be sure to let them be well season'd. Add three quarts of water, two cups of uncooked rice, a good pinch of saffron, and seasonings to taste (salt, pepper, and what you like). Your fire must never slacken for a single Moment, but must be kept up as brisk as possible during the whole time.

As soon as you perceive the chicken and ham to be well stew'd and blended together (about 30 minutes), you must then throw in a can of chick-peas (drained), a cut-up green pepper, and three cut-up tomatoes, and simmer for another two minutes. You will then have only to take a hop, step and jump from your serving-place and you will find yourself in the middle of a First-rate dinner, with all guests at your feet.

Your Olla Podrida may now be consider'd as completely dish'd, fit to set before His Majesty.

"To my mind," Hornbearer replied, "the war between England and France is like a fight between a whale and an elephant. Neither will win, you're fighting for different goals with different battlefields."

He asked whether Audibly thought the war between England and the United States would last much longer. He hoped not, because it was bad for the farmers like himself, who had to leave their farms at inconvenient times, it was bad for the businessmen, because it limited commerce, it was bad for the citizens, who feared for their sons' lives; in short, it was bad for everyone, except the politicians.

"Amen to that, brother," said Jack sincerely. Jack was still turning over in his mind the thought he'd been working on since he'd seen the lumber on the merchantship. He mentioned the immense cost of the building of ships of war, and how they were increasing exponentially as supplies and manpower dwindled. Ships of the line had already run as high as sixty thousand pounds,[14] and costs continued to rise.

"Ah, well," sighed Hornbearer. "I guess you have to spend that money on something. It's how you British keep the peasants as peasants."

Jack didn't quite agree, and thought it was a tactless remark, but Hornbearer quickly went on, as if aware of his *faux pas*. "Do you think we can strike up any private business, you and I?" he asked quietly. "I'd like to discuss a proposition with you at my home tomorrow evening."

Audibly perked up his eyes and ears, but shrugged nonchalantly. "I'd be delighted to hear what you have to propose," he said softly.

When the cloth was drawn and all were sighing with contentment, Mr. Rowan treated them to some outstanding verse, really capital stuff. Captain Hornbearer said he had never heard anything so good.

---

[14] Ed. note: Approximately forty million dollars American by today's equivalent.

Young Men

We are young, hairy, epicene
Oversexed and fat or disgustingly lean
disarmed, charmed, unspeakably silly
Nobody wants the real us
least of all our wives

Our wives are shallow, bubbly, myopic
with bleached hair
Nobody would want them
except for their bodies

It is a crime against manhood
that young people
callow, smug, consciously inconsiderate
should be allowed to prey, prey, prey
and then prey
on a life that has never been lived.

"I regret that I can't return the entertainment," Hornbearer began, "as neither I nor my men have the knack for rhyme. However, Mr. Talbot here knows some excellent poetry, and will recite for you, if you like."

They would like it, of all things, they agreed.

"Mind," said Mr. Talbot, "I didn't write it myself, and I can't claim credits for ought but memory, but here goes:"

Whan that Aprille with his shoures sote
The droghte of Marche hath perced to the rote,
And bathed every veyne in swich licour
Of which vertu engendred is the flour;

When Zephirus eek with his swete breeth
Inspired hath in every holt and heeth

"Oh, for God's sakes!" cried Rowan. "Do speak English, man!"

There was an uncomfortable pause, and then Captain Audibly quickly changed the subject, asking Captain Hornbearer about a game the lads had been engaged in on the deck of Academy, and the talk quickly turned to sports; a subject all present were comfortable with despite the wine, the sillery, and the brandy that had followed. All agreed that it had been a most astoundingly good dinner; Captain Audibly never enjoyed seeing his guests leave dinner on their own two feet and was not disappointed this day, as Captain Hornbearer and his lieutenants were necessarily carried down the ladders and rowed ashore to return to their loving families, singing scolions all the way.

13

It was a fine, brisk and chilly day when Captain Audibly set out for the Hornbearer home. The cat's-paw breeze rippled the surface of the water as Baretta Blondin rowed him in, and the sky was a clear azurean expanse of cloudlessness. He saw no American ships at all until he reached the harbor. He noted with professional interest the two American ships in the harbor. Shortly before the War of 1812 began, the Americans had built a small fleet of ships to protect their merchant ships from the Barbary pirates. They had been building up their navy since, but they did not have many ships of the line yet. There were several frigates, most of which were larger than their British counterparts, and faster than the Royal Navy's ships of the line, but he did not think it would take long before England succeeded in blockading the entire American coast. He recognized the *Montezuma's Revenge*, which the Americans had taken from the Mexicans, who had received it from the Spaniards. The Mexicans had called it *La Cacafiera*, but had not kept it long at all. He studied the new American ship *Drake* with a bit of resentment. Sir Francis Drake had been one of the greatest naval heroes in England's history ("save the beloved Nelson, of course)," Jack thought, touching hand to heart at the thought. Jack Audibly modeled himself after the incomparable Nelson in every possible way, even dressing himself athwartships rather than fore and aft. The first English sailor to circumnavigate the globe, Drake had not only been a most successful buccaneer, a kind of success very dear to Jack's heart, but had defeated the mighty Spanish armada, and had defended in the name of England what the American upstarts now called their country numerous times; had claimed New Albion for Queen Elizabeth, and rescued the colonists from total annihilation in Virginia. His stomach churned at the presumptuous of the Americans to call their new ship *Drake*! His stomach churned also at the thought of the word "buccaneer" which conjured in his mind the smoked meat "boucon" eaten by the pirates of the West Indies, whence derived the word.

As he approached the Hornbearer home, a dalmatian ran across the road in front of him, and his mouth instantly watered for dessert. A flight of geese rose up before him out of a cornfield, honking out a symphony in one-hundred-part harmony, and his heart lifted at the sight of them. He passed a charming blade of grass, undulating sinuously in the breeze, noting that it was green. He passed another charming blade of grass, also undulating sinuously, also green. He passed another, and yet another. If he continued noting them, it would take him the better part of a day to get the half-mile to the Hornbearer home.

He was glad to arrive, at last. His Royal Navy uniform would have been totally inappropriate for the streets of Maryland, but his street clothes were rather tight across his broad chest and shoulders, and his shoes were definitely too tight for the cobbled streets. The Hornbearers had a large plantation, winter corn alternating with fields of tobacco, and a good stand of virgin pine, with chestnut and elm trees lining the path to the manor.

Captain Hornbearer greeted him heartily, and introduced him to the family. Audibly was surprised at the informality with which the women and children were introduced, and regretted that the boy had not the breeding to properly bow to his father's guest, but said nothing. Mrs. Hornbearer greeted him most warmly, expressing gratitude for his having spared her youngest son, and kissed him full on the lips, pressing and scraping her chest to his. He noted, as if from remote, her bathyculpian panting, and wished that Stephen could be there to see her so blissom - Stephen always had something droll to say about Jack's effect on women. He disentangled himself slowly, regretfully, and was greeted by the children. He had already met Clarence, their son; the Hornbearers also had two older sons, but they had already gone to sea earlier in the war. Their niece at some remove, Katie Clydesdale, was about seventeen, and a good image of her aunt in both looks and, apparently, in temperament, although in a much smaller, more petite key, with a fine, straight back, excellent carriage, a mouth much given to laughter and levity, and a youthful radiance. She was small of bosom, as yet, but Jack made a courteous leg, his eyes momentarily vanishing in his broad smile. She was staying with them while her parents were abroad. The youngest child, Elizabeth, could not have been much older than his own swabs Fancy and Carlotta, but she curtseyed prettily, and settled herself next to him as soon as he sat down, admiring his pretty black-and-white Nelson-checquered neckcloth and the crown-and-anchor buttons on his suitcoat, chattering to him about her pet Chesapeake Bay retriever dogs, Artoo and Deetoo. Hearing their names, the dogs bounded up onto Jack. They looked to him like small Newfoundlands; they were dark brown, perhaps five stone beasts, with thick, wavy short coats. He scratched at their backs, for want of anything else to do, and they settled underfoot.

Other guests were present, but they spoke in a dialect he had great difficulty in making out, and it soon became apparent that what they were saying did not merit the effort. In particular, Mr. Sherman, a farmer, had recently moved to the Maryland shore from Norfolk, Virginia, and his regional Norfolk dialect was grating as well as incomprehensible. As they were unable to understand him, either, the conversation soon turned to subjects that clearly excluded him, such as local sports and local customs, and it was only by the dint of sheer willpower that he refrained from dozing off over his apple wine, which was somewhat raw, but very comfortable nonetheless. Hornbearer, noticing his guest's grimace over the wine, called for his houseman.

"Bring up a bottle of the Boone's Farm Apple Wine," he ordered. "The one in the green bottle with the gold twist-off cap... The twist-off cap, mind you."

Jack sat between Mrs. Hornbearer and one of the Americans at dinner, and was uncomfortably aware of the mother's leg pressed hard against his own. He snuck a few longing gazes down Mrs. Hornbearer's gorgeous bosom over a bowl of terrapin soup, and was amply rewarded when she shifted to give him better view, but the thrill of the chase was lacking; he disapproved of froward men and forward women. He glanced at Katie, but she was engaged in an entirely unfeminine discussion with a gentleman to her right, expressing her views aloud, even those contrary to the gentleman's own, and looked not at all at the British captain. He watched her for a while. Her eyes glowed as the first course arrived; she ate her food enthusiastically, disdaining silver at every opportunity, and wrestling with her goose bones with both fists and teeth. She had lovely teeth, Jack noticed. He noticed a great deal more that was lovely of her, unintentionally giving comfort and encouragement to Mrs. Hornbearer, who was much enjoying what she believed to be his reaction to her own probing fingers.

A course of blue crabs followed the goose, and all guests abandoned pretense of civility, dropping the awkward and evidently unaccustomed forks to dig into the feast. Small mallets were provided, but no other implements. The servants did not serve at all; they dumped piles of crabs at various points along the table, and elbows and fists and even knees flew as all grabbed for the largest ones. Jack summoned Quillick, who was waiting just outside, to shell his crabs for him, and was pleased to see Quillick hold his own in the melee, securing a goodly number of the larger specimens, and smashing them ecstatically into smithereens from which the meat could be extracted; bits of shell and seasoning and sauce flying high, but when in Rome, eat the sauce of the gander, as the saying went. There was too little meat to the crabs to be of any use; Captain Hornbearer had a servant lead Quillick off politely, and return to pick the crabs more efficiently, but it was still unsatisfying.

Following the crabs, there was a splendid dish of barbecued pork in a red, tomato-pepper-vinegar sauce, accompanied by plates of unshucked corn with butter sauce, served without any implements. His napkin completely soiled by the crabs, he looked behind him in vain for someone to wipe his hands, but Quillick was elsewhere, and there was no ship's boy to serve. He regretted the mess; he also regretted the barbecue sauce, and reluctantly disentangled his lap from Mrs. Hornbearer, as he could sense that evidence of her adventuresome nature would be all too plainly manifested when they left the table. He had no wish to embarrass Captain Hornbearer; however, that worthy merely glanced in his direction from time to time and shrugged his resignation to the situation—it had clearly arisen many times prior, and would again many times thereafter. The girl Elizabeth played with her dogs under the table, bumping people's feet and crawling over them. He was annoyed by the dogs under the table—it was a habit the Americans must have picked up from their French friends—it would not have surprised him at all had the dogs jumped up to the table to share the plates with the diners.

Conversation was chaotic—there was no order or precedence, no progression of topics, no discipline. The boy, Clarence, spoke out whenever he chose, in a loud and strident tone, and even the girl, Katie Clydesdale, was countenanced to speak her piece aloud when the mood struck her. The guests interrupted each other's dissertations and sentences, and again, Captain Audibly was struck by the emptiness of their thoughts, and the sloppy patterns of speech they exhibited. They were what their Benjamin Franklin (curse him!) would have called nimptopsical, capernoited, cherubimical, but that didn't fully account for their talk or behaviour. Franklin! It struck Jack that even the man's name was blatantly francophilic. Leave it to Benjamin Franklin to come up with two hundred twenty-eight neologisms for drunkenness, but precious few for cleanliness. Like a Frenchman, he couldn't even take a bath right. It was no great marvel that he had caught his death from one of his travesties of a bath. And what utter foolishness to try to save time by tinkering with timepieces! It would not have surprised Jack more had Franklin proposed to make a blanket longer by cutting a piece off one end and sewing it onto the other! Jack's musings passed from Franklin to Jefferson. Jefferson was even worse than Franklin, in that he had had some education and pretensions to culture, and should have known better, but was the most rabid radical of them all, and probably to blame for the whole miserable mess in France, for having praised and supported the fools in the Mob back when it started. He wished fervently for success to Stephen Nattering's mission; how fitting it would be if Nattering's good work with the Creeks in Florida could clear the way to relieve the Americans of the burden of Jefferson's folly in Louisiana; that would take the wind out of old Mr. Jefferson's sails! He returned his attention to the guests, but needn't have, for the quality of their talk. Jack held his tongue for the most of the dinner, only expressing his considered ideas when pressed to do so, and ceasing instantly whenever interrupted. He returned his attention to the girl, Katie. Wandering as his mind did under the bombiliating circumstances, he visualized her lashed to the grating of his ship, being flogged—it was a delightful fancy, and he ran over it several times. He would not have her stripped, modesty forfend; but the thought of her skin and blood flying from her supple, youthful back under the cat-o-nine-tails, with perhaps small chips of bone, as she appeared rather fragile, brought a cheerful, lusty grin to his lips even as he ate.

Dessert was an excellent deep-dish apple pie, with a thick layer of cheddar cheese, accompanied by a bowl of strawberry preserves. Mr. Sherman, who seemed to Jack's mind to be thick-headed as well as coarse, raised his glass after and said, "Here's mud in your eye," to Jack's astonishment, but nothing was flung. Various toasts were proposed and hoisted, and finally, Captain Hornbearer stood with his glass, and announced, "To our President, and your King."

"And to Emperor Napoleon Buonaparte, too, of course," said Mr. Sherman, but Hornbearer withered him with a glance, still standing, and Jack slowly rose to his feet, awkwardly, and suggested amending it, "to all our legitimate rulers, of course."

They drank to that, and then took corn whiskey and Captain Hornbearer's home-brewed applejack brandy in the smoking room.

He inquired, with uncommon delicacy, about the ship *Drake* he had seen; by what prodigious nerve had the Americans named a ship opposed to the British Empire after one of England's greatest heroes?

Captain Hornbearer stared blankly for a moment. "Oh!" he exclaimed. "The *Drake*, of course. No, no, sir, we didn't name that one after Sir Francis Drake at all! It was named after our own Ludwig von Drake."

Audibly was stunned, but held his tongue. He had heard, of course, of the families of mice and ducks in California and Florida that were the objects of a religious cult in America, but could scarcely believe they would name a ship after one of them.

Mr. Sherman delivered himself of a number of ill-worded, ill-thought-out pronouncements concerning the relationships between England and America. He seemed to be working himself up to asking a question; with a sinking heart, Jack divined what it would likely be - the long-standing American preoccupation with the question of Lord Nelson's infirmities. He had heard it several times during his prior voyages to America. His hand flew to his scabbard in anticipation of offense, but he was wearing civilian attire, and felt naked without his sword. He tried to anticipate how Sherman would word his concern; would he hem and haw, feigning delicacy, or would he just blurt it out, as Americans usually did: "Is it true that in addition to having unfortunately lost one arm and one eye, that the man was also monorchid from his injuries in the Battle of St. Vincent?" Fortunately, Captain Hornbearer had the same divination, and intervened and changed the topic before the words were formed; Jack was aware that dueling was outlawed in the colonies following an unpleasantness between Alexander Hamilton and his political rival Aaron Burr—however, he was certain that his marines could easily take a small nearby hill in the name of the Crown, as easy as kiss my hand, and that he could there reach satisfaction against Sherman. But the words remained unspoken, and the uneasy mood of the men slowly dispersed under the soothing influence of brandy.

After the other guests had taken their leave, Captain Hornbearer offered Jack a fat cigar to go with his applejack, and turned to business. He had quite a bit of land in the area; had purchased it on the cheap, and was willing to parcel it to friends almost as cheap - he desired to turn a profit, of course, but values would soon soar - a most prodigiously prime piece of land in the area leading to the Cumberland Gap - it would surely be built up soon, and would be worth its weight in any commodity Audibly cared to mention. Cumberland Gap would of a certainty become the crossroads of American civilization - all roads would lead through it; all commerce would center around that area.

Jack listened to him gravely, his face gradually assuming the look of a dodo, one of the larger, juicier dodos, that sees an Englishman with a treat at no great distance. He was sore tempted, but asked for time to think it over. He was aware that the bulk of his funds was encumbered with an engineer who had called upon him at Cedargrove Cottage with an amazing anti-gravity device; when developed, it would enable thousand-ton ships of the service to elevate and propel despite contrary winds. Dr. Nattering did not think much of the notion, but Jack was aware that Nattering was but an egg in naval matters, with no understanding of the scientific aspects concerned with sailing vessels.

"Time is money," Hornbearer said. "Ye may think on it as long as ye like, until I've sold it to another. When it's gone, it's gone. Buy land, because they ain't making no more of it, t'is the wisest course."

The talk then turned to other commodities. Trade between England and the Colonies was forbidden, but was more than honoured - was venerated -in the breach. Hornbearer raised or had access to beef cattle, tobacco, and pine trees; English interests needed all three. Jack mulled it over—his role as go-between would be easy and lucrative. He agreed to see more of Hornbearer over the next few weeks—not knowing how long he'd be posted to this shore, of course, but expecting to remain for some time to come. Hornbearer mentioned that one of the dinner guests also owned a large stand of good oak, which further interested Jack Audibly. They would discuss it further.

He was certain by now that he wanted to see more of Katie. He was less certain about Mrs. Hornbearer, although it was evident that Captain Hornbearer had long since given up on that battle, and desired only that she be discreet. Discreet. She had not thrown him across the table and jumped on him, but that was about as far as her discretion had carried. During the course of their conversation, Elizabeth had fallen asleep across his lap. Brushing aside Captain Hornbearer's offer to relieve him, he had himself carried her up to her room and put her to bed, savouring the domesticity of the act, missing Sophie and Georges and Fancy and Carlotta terribly. Elizabeth started to awaken as he shifted her into her nightclothes, but he rocked her in the oversized rocking chair in her room, singing her *di petto* a profoundly nautically-influenced version of *Eppie Marlene* in a well-structured baritone, occasionally slipping back into his more comfortable gravelly growly basso profundo, until she fell deeply asleep. He tucked her with her stuffed raggedy doll, and watched Artoo and Deetoo curl up at her feet, longing for his own dear family.

He passed Katie's room, and forgot his family in the longing that the smell of mixed powder, cologne, and girl sweat aroused in him. Mrs. Hornbearer had slipped up the stairs, and pressed herself hard against him in the hallway, leading him into a small dressing chamber. He satisfied himself quickly, firing a very creditable three full rolling broadsides in five minutes and fourteen seconds by his chronometer, (crying out "Diana!" aloud), and her quite incidentally, and returned rapidly to the smoking room, hoping that his extended absence would be attributed to an intestinal aftermath of the dinner. Captain Hornbearer did not comment. Jack took his leave soon thereafter, appointing to meet with Captain Hornbearer again the following afternoon, at a nearby tavern.

* * *

Meanwhile, Stephen Nattering was enjoying surprisingly good success in his endeavor. His contact person in Florida, one Mr. FitzRoy whom he had known as a boy, introduced him to the Creek tribal leaders, who were most grateful for Stephen's gift of three five-gallon carboys of laudanum, along with a supply of the Peruvian coca leaves he had stockpiled for just such a need when last he had been in the southern hemisphere. Although the great Shawnee chief Tecumseh had been killed by the colonists, he had persuaded the Creeks to join in an Indian federation to expel the White colonists from Indian lands. They had only recently celebrated a great victory at Fort Mims, in Alabama, under their Chief Weatherford, and recounted the details long into the night. They had more recently suffered a military setback, but hoped that with replenished arms, they might once again take up the battle. The Creeks recognized a friend to their cause in Nattering, and took him into their encampment. They smoked calumets of marijuana, chewed some of Stephen's khat, and established a very strong liking for the doctor. They described how the White Man had never observed the obligations of their treaties with the Indians, even though the White Men had written them entirely without consultation with Indians; the Creeks believed the aspects of the treaties that were favorable to Indians would <u>never</u> be observed. They cited, for example, the Northwest Ordinance, in which the Americans' Congress had pledged "The utmost good faith shall always be observed towards the Indians; their land and property shall never be taken away from them without their consent, and in their property, rights, and liberty, they shall never be invaded or disturbed... but laws founded in justice and humanity shall from time to time be made, for preventing wrongs being done to them, and for preserving peace and friendship with them..."[15]

The Creeks wondered if these promises would ever be honoured. Stephen expressed judicious doubt, and pledged on

---

[15] The Northwest Ordinance, July 13, 1787, Article Three.

behalf of His Majesty's government that if the Creeks would assist the Crown in regaining the New World lands, the Creeks and all other Indians confederated with them who aided in the war effort would receive fair and equitable treatment from the Empire, including restoration of all lands and properties taken from them by the Colonists. He discussed herbal cures with their medicine man, of course, and introduced that worthy to a rollicking version of the Royal Navy's methods of amputation. The medicine man taught him about unusual herbal teas and poultices to cure various common ailments; Stephen presented him with an alphonsin, the three-armed forceps (invented by Alphonso Ferri, for whom it was named) for extracting bullets from wounds, which gift was very well received.

He was startled by the sight of a young Indian the spitting image of Audibly, but transposed to a ruddier key. It never failed to catch him by surprise when spotting an Audibly look-alike; he had seen them in Yellow in Asia, in darker transpositions in Africa, in male and female versions all along the trade routes, in Canada, in every corner and clime where Britannia ruled the waves, and yet he was taken aback once again. He studied the youth, Rabbit Fitzjackson, carefully. There was no mistake—it was far more resemblance than chance could allow. Rabbit was big of bone, yellow of hair despite being red of face, both by birth and disposition; and Stephen was morally certain that if he examined the boy in a physician's capacity, he would find a set of hairy moles on the left buttock-cheek resembling an archipelago in the shape of the Galapagos. The eyes, the cheekbones, the sweaty oxen neck and general sudor, even the voice was that of his friend. His strong characteristics reminded Stephen of another suspicious youth he had seen that week in the Colonies, Eston Hemings. The boy was something of an outcast in the tribe, as was Igraine, his mother; and Stephen felt for them as he had felt for so many other Audibly outcasts through his travels, from Cedargrove Village to the shores of Botany Bay. He marveled at Audibly's ability to strew his spawn wherever he roamed; wherever wood can swim, there Stephen was sure to find illegitimate Audibly offspring; the chichevache would certainly have fattened on Sophie. Stephen did not approve of Jack Audibly's licentiousness, but nor did he condemn it—he studied it as a naturalist would study any phenomena, more with an eye for understanding it than for altering it. "The Audibly touch," the hands called it, when the captain was out of earshot.

Jack Audibly was the living proof of the wisdom of Jean Baptiste LaMarck, the author of Stephen's beloved *Philosophie Zoologique*, in which he wrote in 1809:

> "In every animal... a more frequent and continuous use of any organ gradually strengthens, develops and enlarges that organ... while the permanent disuse of any organ imperceptibly weakens and deteriorates it, and progressively diminishes its functional capacity, until it finally disappears."

Stephen had no desire for Jack to diminish in his functional capacity, but could occasionally wish for less frequent and especially for less continuous use. He remembered well a conversation they had had concerning minks, whose sexual action could last upwards of eight hours, and the exuberant yet blissful look on Jack Audibly's face at the thought and implied challenge.

During the fourth and fifth day, they concluded their business. The Creeks agreed to consider British suggestions regarding targets within the United States; Stephen agreed to arrange for large quantities of armaments to be delivered in support of Confederate Indian retakings of their own Continent. The following week was spent in naturalist pursuits - they guided him to see pelicans, alligators, bitterns, marlins leaping from the seas, catfish that walked on land, any number of snakes, including three which he felt fully confident would give Jack Audibly the most wondrous anxiety; manatees, and all the rest of the natural history student's fondest dreams come true. Florida was truly the Tir na 'nOg. Although the busk, the green corn harvest feast, had passed, the climate was such that there was constant plenty, and he was feasted every night with the freshest fruits and vegetables, meat, fish and fowl, which he attacked with very hearty appetite, due in part to the *cannabis* (which the Creeks called "wacky tobacky") he partook of nightly. The nightly feasts reminded him of the *calcotada,* the feasts of the green onions grilled over vines and dipped in a romesco sauce,[16] accompanied by wine from the porro, in his native Catalunya. The calcot onions take about a year and a half to grow. When harvested, they are stored in a dry place until they regerminate, at which time they are trimmed and replanted in trenches. After the second growth, they are larger, milder, and sweeter than ordinary scallions, because of the calcot, or shoe of dirt they have worn during their second period of growth. The calcots are grilled over a roaring fire of vines, and then steamed in a wrapping of newspaper, which makes the inside portion tender under the blackened outer layer. When the calcots are finally ready, you grip the root end in one hand, grasp the inner shoots with the other, and pull out the tender center, dip in into the sauce, and slurp it down noisily, dribbling sauce down your chin with glee and boisterous laughter, spurred in no small part by the fine cava and red wine. As the feast continues, the happy Catalunyas enjoy mongetes, botifarra, sangler, cepas, carxofes, and allioli, followed by white botifarra and succulent lamb. Dessert consists of the delightful crema catalana, with its burnt-sugar topping. Stephen tried to describe the feast to his new friends one evening, but as he got carried away by the combination of nostalgia and whatever he was smoking other than tobacco, he lapsed more and more into his native Catalan tongue, quite incomprehensible to the Creeks, until finally an impatient youngster burst out in Spanish "Si eres Espanol, habla cristiano!" This breach of etiquette so disturbed the elders that a noticeable pall hung over the remainder of the evening's festivities.

All in all, however, it was completely idyllic; his business done, he had the leisure he never got to enjoy when Audibly prodded him with his eternal "Not a moment to be lost!" He wondered briefly if it had been wise to leave Dravis behind; although he could be a

---

[16] The sauce is made of ground roasted almonds and hazelnuts, garlic cloves, and tomatoes, simmered in olive oil, with vinegar and hot pepper added towards the end

confounded nuisance, Stephen was aware that Dravis oft-times suffered from an incongruously delicate digestion, and that he was not liked by his shipmates; he wondered if anyone would feed Dravis loblolly with the little spoon in the sick-berth; but such questions soon slipped from his mind. He even got to see a panther!

14

Jack was called aboard *Cuchulainn*, Commodore Spring's flagship, and received assignment to the fleet blockading a portion of the mid-Atlantic. Spring acknowledged Audibly's requirement to pick up Nattering; the assignment would be supplemental to the fleet's actions, rather than sole responsibility for a sector falling to *Aghast*. He was delighted with the news of Napoleon's abdication and exile to Elba; as soon as the signal went out from the *Cuchulainn* his dear *Aghast* responded with a barrage of cannon fire.

They wore on and off, but there was little action. In the afternoon, he was rowed ashore for his appointment with Captain Hornbearer.

He noticed the usual gaggle of girls clustering around the gig as he alit, but paid them little mind. One of them, with the typical braying voice of the young girls who frequent the shores of all countries when naval vessels come in, was cavorting in a most unfeminine fashion, displaying an occasional flash of ankle and even a glimpse of her farthingale.[17] Her languorous drawl was loud, offensive to his ears; she was eyeing the British men with interest, and finally worked up the nerve to jerk her thumb in Quillick's direction as she addressed her remarks to Baretta Blondin: "What o, sailor!" she asked, quite happy now, with a few tots of gin under her narrow belt. "Can he dance, mate?"

Her friend pulled her back, indignantly. "Jane, you ignorant sloth! I saw him first!"

Jane flushed, and then reared her head:

"You stop your gob!" she exclaimed angrily. "I may be ignorant, but at least I"m not fat! You"re so fat, if you ever went swimming in the ocean, Spain would claim you as a New World!"

---

17   The Reader's imagination is challenged as to the etymological origins of the name of this feminine garment.

"So what?" retorted Lilith. "You're so ignorant, you'd have to put rouge on your forehead to make up your mind!"

Baretta Blondin turned away, embarrassed, but Quillick pulled at his forelock with unusual shyness, and listened openly, eagerly to the dispute.

Jack did not wait to hear the outcome. On his way to the tavern, he passed a herd of gaseous cows, and as he hummed, one of the ruminants uttered two phrases of its own, and then began a dialogue with the others of the herd. The sky lowered; the cows lowed back.

Audibly and Hornbearer greeted each other warmly; they had more in common than in difference. They spoke of naval affairs of their two countries, the traditional and the modern thoughts, over oyster soup, quail, ham baked in the Virginia style, fresh porgies, succotash, and wines. America had a standing navy now, but its future was cloudy. Captain Hornbearer hoped it would not be disbanded after the skirmish with England ended, because a country without a navy was at the mercy of the world. Captain Audibly agreed wholeheartedly.

"Your Thomas Jefferson, a genius in many fields, is mistaken in this," Audibly suggested in a manner he hoped would not be taken amiss. He disliked criticizing his host's leaders, but had strong feelings about naval matters. "Ye'll always need a professional navy," he said. "Even way back—the Greek city-state of Athens had a government-supported, organized navy, to protect against the Persians. The Byzantine Empire at Constantinople would have fallen to the Moslems had they not had a professional navy commanding the seas to protect themselves from the Turks, Saracens and Vandals, and they lasted a thousand years due to that navy. We'll not always be at odds—your people are my people, and when your President comes to his senses, and you are reunited with Canada under our Empire, your strong navy will be our bastion on this side of the world. I know you don't have a permanent, professional army or navy, as we do, but ye'll always have need for both in support of the Empire."

"Ye'll not win this war," Hornbearer said quietly. "But let's not argue that today. I'd like your advice on setting up a training academy for our future naval officers—I've been working on it for some time, hoping to see something established here on the Chesapeake bay, perhaps in Annapolis. What think ye?"

Audibly was of two minds on the subject. Traditionally, navy men were trained at sea, as midshipmen from the age of thirteen or even earlier. But it was a haphazard process, at best - a professional academy would have merits, as long as the men coming out had had at-sea practice, and would not supplant those who had come up the right way, he could see that they could be a valuable supplement to the corps - perhaps they could receive their training in mathematics and navigation on land, and enter at sixteen as midshipmen with a requirement of four years experience for making lieutenant instead of entering at thirteen requiring six years. It could work. The men could perhaps spend a year in the Royal Navy, learning to do things right, interspersed perhaps after the first year of academy training, and then return with the experience to receive more classroom training.

Captain Hornbearer lowered his voice. "I owe you an explanation for my wife's behaviour." Audibly started to protest, but Hornbearer overrode him.

"I betrayed my wife early in our marriage, and she found out of it. It was the way I was—it was no more uncommon in the American navy than in the English, but the women here are different. She's been getting back to me in kind ever since. Frankly, I find it almost a convenience that she takes it that way. It frees me to do what I long to do when in ports, and she's an excellent and lusty wife in all regards. We try not to rub each other's noses in it, but we've come to an accommodation on the subject that suits us both."

Jack considered on it for a while. He was grateful that his Sophie did not feel that way, because he had not been entirely faithful to her himself, including on this voyage, of course; although he tried his best not to respond to the women he seemed to attract wherever he went, yet he could not bear the thought of

Sophie lying with another man. He felt bad for Captain Hornbearer for having to tolerate his wife's infidelity as the price of his own; Jack didn't think it ought to work that way; and it was physically evident that the two children he had seen did not resemble the father or the mother in the slightest.

Hornbearer sighed softly, and continued, "Samuel Rogers once said 'It doesn't much signify whom one marries, for one is sure to find next morning that it was someone else.'" Audibly considered, and thought it very true. There had been a great many times since his marriage that he had woken up beside someone else.

They spoke little of the land deals that they had discussed the previous night—Audibly was not ready to commit large sums of money to yet another land purchase, however excellent, and had little to invest at the moment anyhow, at least until the merchantships he had taken were condemned. As to brokering the commodities, he could give no response until he returned to England and lined up the proper buyers. He thought perhaps the income from the brokering could finance the land purchase, and Hornbearer agreed in principle, although he was obviously in some rush to sell some parcels—he had perhaps over-committed his own resources in his certainty that Cumberland Gap would inevitably someday be the greatest city in America. Jack nibbled on pats of butter as they spoke, and they finished their meeting with a handsome cheesecake topped with caramelized apple slices. Jack declared that although the food was excellent, it was nowhere to touch the quality of the fare he had consumed at the Hornbearer home the previous night.

"I wonder if ye might clarify something that had me mystified last night," Jack asked.

"By all means," replied Hornbearer, leaning forward.

"What meant your guests by the word 'yawl?'" Jack asked. "In England, we mean by it a small, two-masted craft, rigged fore-and-aft. I heard it referred to several times by your guests, but they seemed to mean something entirely else?"

129

Captain Hornbearer was puzzled. "Why, that's indeed what we mean by it, too: a small jolly boat with a short mizzenmast astern of the rudder post. I guess I didn't hear the term you mean last night at all, so I don't know the context in which you heard it. By the by, do you like the cheesecake? Would y'all like some coffee?"

The coffee was steaming hot, and just the thing for the cheesecake. Afterwards, Jack stood and raised his glass.

"To a long, bloody war, and the sickly season," he exclaimed. Hornbearer had half-stood, but froze at the words.

"I mean," Jack started, but paused, nonplused by Hornbearer's reaction. He half tried to say "To peace," but the words stuck in his craw.

Both men were disconcerted, half-standing, glasses at half-mast.

"Well," Hornbearer finally said, "here's looking at you." They drained their glasses to that, awkwardly.

They were annoyed to hear a group of rowdy, drunken sailors, whooping it up in a corner of the dining room, singing at the tops of their inebriated lungs. Hornbearer's heart sank when they started, knowing that they would inevitably turn to *The Hornet and the Peacock*, by far the most popular drinking song in the colonies. He did not have long to wait: the sailors sang it with rousing gusto.

> Ye Demos, attend, and ye Federals, too
> I'll sing you a song that you all know is true,
> Concerning the *Hornet*, true stuff, I'll be bail
> That rumpled the *Peacock* and lowered her tail.

> "Sing hubber, O bubber," cried Old Granny Wale,[18]
> "The *Hornet* can tickle the British bird's tail.
> Her stings are all sharp and they'll pierce without fail.
> Success to our navy!" cried Old Granny Wale.

Hornbearer glanced apprehensively at Captain Audibly. Audibly's hackles were raised, his face turning purple.

---

18 From "Granuaille," the Irish word for an old woman.

This bird it was bred in the land of King George
Her feathers were fine and her tail very large;
She spread forth her wings like a ship in full sail
And prided herself in the size of her tail.

King George, he then says "To America go
The *Hornet,* the *Wasp* is the British king's foe.
Pick them up, my dear bird, spread your wings to the gale."
"But beware of those insects," cries Old Granny Wale.

"Pay them no mind," said Hornbearer. "Sailors will take a dram when they get ashore, as ye ken." Jack reluctantly removed his hand from his waist, where his sword would have been had he been properly dressed.

"Might I ask you for another clarification?" Jack asked, darkly. "What did Sherman mean last night by 'here's mud in your eye?' Was he making sport of Lord Admiral Nelson's infirmity?"

"I'm sure it never crossed his mind—certainly it never crossed mine—it's just something we say when we have nothing else to say. Is it the same with the long and bloody war?"

"No, no, indeed," replied Jack. "I meant that with all my heart." His voice tailed off, as he realized what Hornbearer must be thinking.

Away flew this bird at the word of command,
Her flight was directed to freedom's own land;
The *Hornet* discovered her wings on the sail,
And quickly determined to tickle her tail.

So at it they went, it was both pick and sting,
The *Hornet* still working keen under her wing.
"American insects," quoth she, "I'll be bail,
Will humble the king bird and tickle her tail."

Hornbearer was on his feet, proposing a toast. Jack did not respond at all, staring at the sailors with bulging eyes, bulging veins standing out on his neck. Hornbearer quietly retrieved two buttons that had popped off Audibly's shirt.

The *Peacock* now mortally under her wing
Did feel the full force of the *Hornet*'s sharp sting;
She flattened her crest like a shoal on the whale,
Sunk down by her side and lowered her tail.

Success to brave Lawrence, who well knew the nest
Where the *Hornet* and *Wasp* with honor still rest.
We'll send them a force, and with skill, I'll be bail,
We'll humble King George, and tickle his tail.

"Sing hubber, O bubber," cried Old Granny Wale,
"The *Hornet* can tickle the British bird's tail.
Her stings are all sharp and they'll pierce without fail.
Success to our navy!" cried Old Granny Wale.

As the sailors departed, repeating the chorus and bellowing with laughter, Jack slowly settled back in his seat, his anger fading, replaced by dejection. He drained his brandy in a gulp, and apologized to Hornbearer for his reactions.

"No need at all," Hornbearer assured him. "I'm sure that if my navy had lost as many battles as yours, I'd be hipped about it too."

Captain Hornbearer presented Jack with some magnificent gifts: a bearskin rug, and a beautiful fox stole for his wife, whom Hornbearer declared must be a most lovely woman.

Captain Audibly admitted that Sophie was far, far better of character and spirit than he merited, and brought out some gifts for Hornbearer: a jeweled scabbard from India, and an exotic-smelling collection of spices. "Mrs. Hornbearer sets such a lovely table," he smiled, "I'm sure she'll do honour by these flavourings from our dominion to the East."

Each thanked the other profusely, and indeed, each was touched by the gifts they had received. Hornbearer asked a favour of

Audibly —"When you get back to England, and God willing you'll fare safely, please remember me to Admiral Tarte, whom I met some years ago and was well-taken with, and please convey my very fondest thoughts to his lovely wife, Molly."

"I'll do so gladly," replied Jack. "I'm sure to see them soon after landing."

"I'm sure you will," Hornbearer thought to himself, but said nothing but his gratitude, and expressed his hope for continued friendship, howsoever the war turned; Jack concurred warmly and sincerely.

They parted with the knowledge that although their countries were at war, and they might be required very soon to harm each other, there was a mutual respect between them, an increased understanding of each other's perspectives, a deepening friendship, and a likely business partnership in the offing. Jack suggested with the sincerest bonhomie that should Captain Hornbearer find himself in Mother England after the ruckus ended, that Hornbearer should be sure to visit with him and meet his dear wife, Sophie. Hornbearer's eyes seemed to gleam at the prospect, and he assured Captain Audibly most emphatically that he should dearly love to visit, and meet the charming wife.

Jack Audibly was delighted beyond ecstasy upon returning to the *Aghast* to find a note from Katie Clydesdale. There would be a dance on Friday evening, and she hoped he could attend, because she wanted him to meet a particular friend of hers, a young woman of twenty-two years of age; Miss Mary Challans, who was, through no fault of her looks, unattached; a dreadful fate at that age. Katie hoped that Captain Audibly would be just the man to entertain the lady, and perhaps bring her out of her shell of shyness into a more sociable attitude.

Jack snatched up a handful of saltcellars, biscuits, and implements, and began laying out his campaign for winning Katie's heart and favours.

* * *

In Florida, meanwhile, Stephen Nattering was having a most delightful interlude. He saw the panther (*fels concolor coryi*) again, marveling at its sandy brown coat, its snowy white belly, and the delightful small black line down the middle of its head. It must have been seven feet long, and he thought it went nearly twelve stone. He ate fresh oranges and grapefruits daily, and Takesgun, the medicine man, introduced him to the most delightful hallucinogenic mushrooms he had ever encountered. Takesgun recognized, as a doctor would, Nattering's weakness for mind-altering substances, and steered him away from the most dangerous; yet there were more than enough of the milder forms to enable a wide expanse of experiences. They fished, hunted, and trapped for their dinner daily, often with Rabbit Fitzjackson, who benefited by Stephen's attention as a means of apprenticing himself to Takesgun; naturalizing and botanizing all the while, and Stephen felt his strength and energy rising under the freedom from time and care. He marveled at the Indians' perspective on the plant kingdom. Stephen had previously concentrated more on the animal kingdom, on the birds, on the insects, than he had on the plants; not from lack of interest in the plant kingdom, but because one could only do so much. Now, however, he was reawakening as to a whole new world. Within his pantheon of heroes, the Frenchman Cuvier stood high. Cuvier, himself, however, had adopted the techniques of LaMarck as partial foundation for his theories. LaMarck had been a distinguished botanist before ever he began his study of the animal kingdom, basing his zoological research on his botanical learnings and techniques. Under Takesgun's tutelage, Stephen explored a new world of wonder that he had sadly neglected in the past. As LaMarck had discovered families within the trees, i.e., similarities between the families of maples, pines, oaks, etc., and had extended that to his theories of families within the animal kingdom; so Stephen focused his attention on the ferns and fronds, the brushes, the rich, green leaves on Florida trees and bushes, and was as a child in his explorations of discovery.

It was possible, he mused, that had his command of French been better, he might have become a botanist rather than an ornithologist, if only he had read *Flore francaise* earlier in his formative years. LaMarck's theories were revolutionary, discredited by many, but to Stephen, undeniably true. The notion that changes produced in the individual plant or animal as the result of its response to environment may be transmitted to the offspring, and thus lead to progressive changes and thence to the evolution of new species was heretical; yet Stephen believed it to be not only possible, but true. How fortunate that he had so recently completed his first reading of *Philosophie zoologique* as to have the ideas dancing in his brain in confluence with his fortunate encounter with Takesgun!

They conversed all through the day, about whatever came to mind. As the weather was getting warmer, especially at mid-day, Stephen asked Takesgun, "How do you deal with overreactions to the enormous heat in Florida?"

"With herbal infusions," replied Takesgun. "I'll point out the barks and leaves as we pass them." He did so, and asked Stephen the same question: "As your British tars are frequently unused to hotter climes, how do you deal with them?"

"Usually, I bleed them as we approach the warmer latitudes. When my Captain arrives in a few days, I'll demonstrate for you, and you may wish to try your hand at it while he's here, too."

Stephen discussed with him the theories of LaMarck, and solicited the medicine man's opinions, and was much pleased to receive the most thoughtful, reasonable support for his own thinkings on the subject. "I once had the honour of speaking with LaMarck," Stephen offered, "at a Royal Society dinner in honour of Sir Joseph Banks' return from Australia."

"Really!" responded Takesgun. "What did the great man say to you?"

"Oh, and not much," answered Stephen. "He said, 'Donnez-moi le sel, s'il vous plait.'"

Takesgun waited for a translation, but Stephen was nodding off at the pleasant recollection, and Takesgun did not care to intrude.

The climate was agreeably mild, the colours were most amazing, and the vegetation, to say nothing of the life it supported, was infinite in its variety.

15

Captain Audibly was in a fine frame of mind Friday. He wished Dr. Nattering were aboard to help him. Nattering had a supply of cantharides, the Spanish Fly aphrodisiac, which Jack could not locate, and demurred at asking the loblolly boy to give him. He had never used such a drug on a woman before, but wished he had some tonight, just in case opportunity arose for it. He tried to recall what he knew about other aphrodisiacs, but it had been twenty-five years since he had been a midshipman, and even then had never had a use for philters, never until now. He remembered ambergris, the waxy substance from the intestines of sperm whales, but that didn't seem appropriate or accessible at this time. The Persians, those generous sensualists, had put particular reliance in the cloves; he could no doubt get cloves from Quillick; and perhaps some savory, the personal emblem of the satyrs, those insatiable lechers of Greek mythology; or perhaps basil, which the Italian writer Boccaccio had believed to be a symbol of love. He finally decided against the notion—he would take his chances as he had always done, nearly always successfully.

Quillick double-scraped his cheeks until they burned fiery red; and laid out his best evening-coat without complaint: swallow-tails, cummerbund, shoes shining like looking-glasses; and of course, his best Nelson-checquered bow-tie. Quillick was secretly pleased that the rendezvous would take place on American soil, so there would be no question of the Captain wearing out his number one scraper. Jack considered various breeches-stuffers, but rejected them. He had never stuffed his breeches with anything but himself, and himself had always served; he was always amazed at the success other men had flying under false flags, but was satisfied with his Union Jack. Mr. Rowan would accompany him, to intercept Miss Mary Challans and otherwise run interference for his captain, as necessary. He was delighted to do so - a happy captain made for a happy ship, and a happy Captain Audibly made for a very happy ship, indeed, since he was of a genial nature at most times anyway, and his affability merited whatever effort was required.

They appeared at the door of Mrs. Fellington-Smythering's home at the first toll of eight; Katie and Miss Challans stopped giggling as the tall, broad-shouldered officers entered, their generous expanse of shirt-fronts as white as their gloves seemingly filling the doorway. Katie led Miss Challans up, shyly, and presented her to the two bowing gentlemen.

Jack did not feel so grim now, when the mantle-clock struck eight, for now the action was engaged, the time of waiting was over, he was on the enemy's deck at last.

"Captain Audibly, you look quite splendid; may I present my particular friend, Miss Mary Challans?"

"Ha-h'm, ha-h'mmmm," Audibly replied. Katie was absolutely smashing. She wore a gown of a shade that had previously been etched in his mind as "Diana-blue;" now that colour would ever after have a new name. The gown had a high bodice, and demure, girlish pink ruffles about the edges, but the blue brought out her eyes, and her sparkle. It was not diaphanous enough to please him, but the soft fabric clung to her girlish bends and curves. He quickly recovered, as sea-captains do, and bowed deeply. "Miss Clydesdale, Miss Challans, how utterly enchanting you both appear - may I present my lieutenant, Mr. Daniel Rowan?" Jack gazed longingly at Katie's diminutive bosom, trying to fathom through the material of her dress its approximate size, shape, and firmness. Recalling his manners, he tried to simulate a comparable ogle at Miss Challans' offering which, although definitely larger, was equally definitely amorphous.

Rowan made a most presentable leg, gazed directly into Miss Challans' eyes, offered her his arm, and led her away, never taking his eyes from hers.

Jack offered Katie his arm. Her breathing was ragged as she took it, and she trembled as he led her onto the dance floor. The quartet was beginning a waltz, and she felt ethereal in his arms.

Sensing her anhelation, he did not attempt to pull or press her, but allowed her free rein, and she melted into him, taking short steps to his longer ones on her initial backing; longer steps to his shortened ones as she advanced. Their legs brushed; she seemed to have difficulty breathing. He let her explore the feeling, and although she occasionally lost the step or trod him, she was lighter than air, and he had difficulty in maintaining a comforting chatter as they danced the night away. She made a remark; he chuckled at it, his chest heaving against her cheek, and they chuckled together at everything and nothing. He discoursed on the music; she told him secrets about some of the guests present, sniffing his chest from time to time, sometimes weakening in her legs so that he had to support her. He nuzzled her hair; heaven must smell like that, he thought. Something changed within her as she sniffed at him—she couldn't identify it, but she felt the transition, and knew it was natural.

One of the matronly chaperones looked suspiciously at the discrepancy between their ages, and started to approach. Rowan loomed, and asked the dowager for directions to the punch bowl; by the time he and Mary Challans disengaged from her path, Jack and Katie were on the far side of a knot of dancing bodies, cheek to cheek, eye locked on eye, breathing shallowly as one.

Jack glanced around, positioning them so that he had the weather-gauge of all the chaperones. One of those worthies was glaring in his direction, fluttering her hands in dismay. But, he felt, in case signals can neither be seen nor perfectly understood, no captain can do very wrong if he places his ship alongside that of the enemy.

He noted from the corner of his eye her cousin Clarence Hornbearer, wrestling with another lad his age to impress the young girls surrounding them; the other young man was clearly stronger, but Clarence had technique, and pinned the larger youth; although the girls seemed not to care that much about his victory—they helped the larger boy to his feet, and brought him punch and cookies.

He caught sight of Rowan and Mary. Rowan was reciting poetry; Miss Challans was smiling happily, winking and giggling to Katie.

Jack and Katie fed each other chocolates and candied violets from a tray, laughing. She found his exquisite politeness quaint, but endearing. They walked in the garden, wordlessly chuckling at the world. He liked the feel of her chuckle against his arm; he hummed the Mozart andante the quartet was playing, and she pressed her cheek to his chest, enjoying the rumbling vibration of his hum.

He kissed her gently, barely grazing her lips with his own, so as not to alarm her, but she was already past alarm.

"Kiss me hearty," she moaned. Jack practically swooned at the remark.

"You're an admirer of Nelson!" he exclaimed happily.

"Whaaa?" she was puzzled by the remark.

"A girl after my own heart!" he declared. "I've never met any woman who quoted from Admiral Nelson before. I'm an admirer of his, too. You and I have so much in common. We were meant for each other. It's destiny!"

"Kismet?" she asked, incredulously. "Hardly," she responded.

Jack was again weak-kneed. "I can't believe it," he gushed. "A Nelson fan through and through. I am his biggest fan. I even dress myself athwartships rather than fore and aft, as he did."

"Don't show me," she blushed deeply, but then held his hand against her pounding heart.

He made no moves against her; to his own astonishment, he found himself thinking of his Fancy and Carlotta, wondering how long it would be before some blackguardly viper would be eyeing them, dancing with them, chuckling against them; his heart panged him, and he disentangled himself from the young girl Katie.

They continued to walk, but he felt uneasy, and maintained a reserved distance from her eagerness. They returned to the ballroom; they danced, but she could sense that he was more remote. She ran through everything she had said or done, and could not figure out what had happened. A rainwater-soft tear ran down her cheek; he wiped it away with a finger, smiled at her, and they danced anew; a lively gavotte, something wild-eyed, what Stephen had once called a *rinnce fadha*, which the Colonists called a "Virginia reel"—Jack had no trouble with the steps, of course; it was something akin to the Sir Roger de Coverley or the Dorset four-hand reel, but rowdier, noisier, less elegant. They danced a stately pavane, and a lively gigue, her eyes flashing like comets; she tried to rub against him, but he chuckled and held her off. He told her how extraordinarily lovely she was; her hair, her eyes, her dress, her shoes, her manner—it was completely true; he was near tears himself, but couldn't bear to advantage himself with her. He wondered if age was finally catching up with him; he suddenly felt intimations of mortality; but when he looked at Katie, he saw Carlotta. He resolved to write to Sophie immediately; to warn her to have a talk with the girls—it was never too early to warn little girls about the vile machinations of men—as Dr. Nattering always said, "Forewarned is half an octopus."

One of the local young gentlemen approached behind him, looking to cut in; Jack wishing for his press-crew to suddenly materialize. He bent forward, dipping Katie Clydesdale. When he arighted her, Daniel Rowan was grinning at him; the local was flabbergasted to find Miss Mary Challans happily waltzing in his arms, reveling in her new-found popularity. Jack observed that there were more unattached ladies than gentlemen in the room, wartime conditions; he nodded permission to Rowan, but Rowan stood aloof, declining to sport while he had the watch.

Jack danced on with Katie, but felt haggard. He caught Rowan's eye, and they handed the ladies into a carriage, and returned to the *Aghast*.

He sniffed at the wind on the ship, and glanced at the riggings and sails, but his heart was sore. He turned in, despondently, worrying about the responsibilities a naval captain had for the whole goddammed world, wondering at what point his youth had deserted him, leaving him with an aging body and a dispiritedness; he slept.

He heard, as through his dreams, a boat hooking on, Blondin's voice saying "Mind the paint, handsomely, handsomely now," and then Quillick tapped and entered his cabin, clearing his throat firmly and noisily.

"And if you're quite decent, that's good now, for here's a lovely young lady here to see you," and then Katie was in his cabin, standing beside his bed, eyes wide with trepidation and daring, cheeks flaming—no cosmetic could approach that—her lovely neck flushed; and then slipping into it, under his sheet. He kissed her eyes, and breathed her scent—talcum and musk. He moved not at all then, but allowed her to accustom herself to the feel of him, the sound of his breath, his spice. She explored him, questing, foraging; he made reassuring sounds, but did not want to frighten her by yielding to his own needs and desires. She was timid of the deed, but not of the man. When he finally judged the time to be right, he was tender, sensitive, patient. As the ship swayed and rocked, he crossed her 't,' raking her gently with his full broadside. She slept, then, sucking her fore and middle fingers with her other fingers curled around her chin. He removed her fingers from her mouth, and replaced them with his own. She sucked gently on his finger, and he sucked on hers, so very salty, so very sweet. He watched her sleep, listened to her breathe, and felt himself young again. As the sun rose over the mainsail mast, his own mainsail mast rose, and he dotted her 'i,' double-charged and double-shotted.

It was time to pick up Doctor Nattering. As they weighed the anchor, the men straining at the capstan, the captain's usual profanity sounding uncharacteristically like benisons, he gazed at her skiff with his glass, she waving his "*N*"-embroidered handkerchief to him, until the little boat was quite out of sight, and longer.

He declined Quillick's proffered coffee, and refused breakfast, wanting to taste Katie forever.

16

They were favored by a sweet, mild breeze for the return to Florida. Tom Pushings and James Mowell had returned on the packet in the night, and Captain Audibly was glad to have his lieutenants back, although sorry for Rowan's consequent drop in status, sorry indeed in light of the fine way Rowan had blocked for him the previous evening. They passed an occasional prize ship headed for Canada or the West Indies, but the seas were fairly empty. The blockade was effective primarily as a deterrent to merchant activity; England had not enough ships to spare for a proper blockade in the west Atlantic, but merchants were more hesitant to risk their ships being taken by the occasional Royal Navy cruiser, so the blockading effect was almost as good as if there had been many more ships. Most of the prizes that had been taken on the incoming leg had held slaves; these vessels were sent to Canada, both crew and cargo glum at the prospect of a tour of duty in His Majesty's Navy. The crew would have the better time of it, as they would be rated able seamen and treated decent if they bent to; the slaves would regain the strength that had sapped on the voyage to the new world when they would be treated to the salt pork, pease porridge, salt beef, and ship's biscuit they would receive, and although untrained in reefing and handing, they could learn to pull on a rope quickly enough. Jack thought they were fortunate to have been taken by the English—they'd be fairly useless for a while, but if they survived the tour, they could expect their freedom at some time in the future; the sea cruise would most certainly be preferable to plantation life, and they would be exposed to a discipline and civilization they could not have received in their native Africa. They would acquire punctuality, cleanliness, and naval sobriety. England had its responsibilities. The outgoing prizes predominantly carried molasses, or tobacco, or whiskey; those they encountered south of the Carolinas had been sent to the West Indies; Jack did not think there was lucrative prize in the area, but one could never tell, and the two merchantmen he had already taken would add to his coffers nicely, and he was proud to be part of the force blockading his enemy's trade so apparently successfully.

The *Aghasts* were quite surprised to find Dr. Nattering at the appointed place at the appointed time. After searching the doctor for wildlife and releasing the two quite small alligators over the doctor's protests ("For heaven's sakes, Mr. Blondin, don't you appreciate the noble *crocodylidae loricate!*"), Blondin carried him through the swamp and placed him in the gig, and brought him onto the *Aghast*. After asking each other if he was indeed himself, and had he indeed come to this place, Jack and Stephen talked quietly through the night, and the next morning, the crew began unloading the three crates of muskets and ammunition, the crate of rum, and the assorted supplies and personal gifts for the Creeks. It was unseasonably hot by the time they were back in the swamp. Audibly, empty-handed except for his ceremonial sword, tried not to sweat in front of Stephen as he marched through the mangroves, but his full dress uniform, which Stephen insisted upon for the stature it would lend to the agreements that had been reached during the previous fortnight, was quite heavy, and his face soon shone as red as that of Rabbit Fitzjackson, who stared agape at Audibly as he would have stared at a ghost. Jack Audibly had never been to Florida before, alas, but he was quick to notice that it possessed all the thermal advantages of the Sahara Desert without the drawback of low humidity. He pondered this as he watched the steam rising from his boot-tops. Stephen pitied Jack his sweaty neck, but could not purge him until they had achieved some privacy, which was not likely for hours to come. Stephen reflected on a witticism he had recently heard: "Horses sweat, men perspire, but ladies glow." He mused as he strode on, watching rivulets course down Jack's back, hearing Jack's toes sloshing in his boots, "sure, and Jack Audibly's diaphoresis transcends whatever one might say about horses. Horses are Saharan in comparison."

On the outskirts of the Creek encampment, edged to the verdant forest, an elder sage of the tribe contemplated the approaching procession. By his side his grandson, a sharp-eyed lad of six summers (there being no winters in this clime) tended a caged lizard—a child destined, it may be added, for dismemberment by the Americans some short six years hence, for offenses of a sexual nature.

"Grandpapa," said the sweet child. "I see a palatine, a sumptuous palatine of huge, enormous girth, approaching! Although he is ornate to a high degree, he is sweating very like a fevered horse. He is as red of face as you or I. And the man who dabbles in feces is beside him, entreating him onward step by step."

"They are foreign devil barbarians, my child. They are a file of the uncivilized beasts from across the sea. They overcook their vegetables, and sneer and curse at the nation of fine chefs and gourmet delights to their southeast."

"I desire to observe the large one as he eats," begged the child.

"There is absolutely no doubt in my mind that you shall have ample opportunity for observation of same," replied the sage, withdrawing his attention from the Englishmen as they reached the encampment.

"Namaste, kemo sabe," Jack greeted the Creeks. They rushed to fan him, to ply him with beverages, to relieve him of his heavy coat, they were alarmed at his appearance of being on the point of heatstroke; but when they had seen to his comfort, they welcomed him and his gifts.

They ate oranges at the Indian encampment, sweet and sticky and utterly refreshing. The Creeks were suitably impressed with Captain Audibly's uniform and stature, and had him to wind his chelengk several times, laughing gleefully at its tinkly tune. They were also impressed with the weaponry, politely inquiring about the availability of Sir William Congreve's newest rockets; disappointed that there had been none on board the *Aghast*, and hoping that some could be made available in the future. The muskets were quite acceptable, however, far superior to the muzzle-loading blunderbusses and matchlocks they had been using; and they spent the remainder of the afternoon sighting and practicing with them, which activity kept Takesgun and Stephen fully occupied in their professional capacity well into the evening.[19]

After the evening feast, the Creeks entertained the Englishmen on their tom-toms, and Jack reluctantly shared their calumet, careful not to inhale too deeply, but not willing to offend his hosts, either. The Indians had many questions about traditional European warfare, and were completely at sea concerning naval affairs. Stephen Nattering had apparently abandoned his usual reticence during his visit, and had filled their ears with tales of his noble captain; how the captain had advised Nelson on strategy at Trafalgar (based, of course, on what Stephen had earlier taught him about tactics); and he had distinctly placed Audibly as a third lieutenant in both *Colossus* and *Orion* during the Battle of St. Vincent's. Jack was embarrassed for the sake of Nattering for having so grievously blundered in his account as to place him on two ships simultaneously; Stephen sought to play it off lightly as a mathematical error with a quip: "As well you know," he cackled, "there are three kinds of people in the Royal Navy: those who can count and those who can't." Jack waited for the punch-line, but as it didn't come, he sang *To Anacreon in Heaven* to distract the Indians from Stephen's gaffe:

> The yellow-hair'd god, and his nine fusty maids
> To the hill of old Lud will incontinent flee.
> Idalia will boast but of tenantless shades,
> And the biforked hill a mere desert will be.
>
> My thunder, no fear on't
> Will soon do its errand,

---

[19] Historical note: The muskets were particularly needed, as the Creeks had just the previous fortnight suffered heavy defeat, along with their Cherokee allies. The Creek Civil War continued, even as they fought against the Americans, who were assisted by the rebelling factions.

And dam'me! I'll swinge the ringleaders, I warrant.
I'll trim the young dogs, for thus daring to twine,
The myrtle of Venus with Bacchus' vine.

To Stephen's dismay, they set out at moonlight to return to *Aghast*; he had wanted to show Jack some fascinating flora of the region, and the spoor of the panther; but Jack insisted that there was not a moment to lose, and he would not for all the panther spoor in the New World miss the morning tide. The doctor muttered to Reverend Martinet that had Copernicus sailed on a Royal Navy ship, he'd have realized quickly that the earth and the sun and the moon and the stars all revolved around the whims of a naval captain. Stephen in his professional judgment thought Audibly should rest at least overnight, because despite Stephen's guidance and several rounds of practice on the ship's boys, Takesgun had somewhat botched his bleeding, missing the vein not once but twice, Jack's vein being somewhat harder to find in its fleshy mass than that of a small boy. Takesgun had had to abandon the lancet, and complete the job with a horse-fleam. Rabbit Fitzjackson, meanwhile, exulting in his new role as apprentice to the medicine man, was also permitted to practice bleeding on the ship's boys, and did a fairly creditable job for his first time. He was younger than many of the boys, but none of them would disobey the captain's order by refusing an arm, and he soon got the hang of it. He was delighted with Stephen's parting gifts to him: a trepan (and hurried instructions on its use), a clyster-pipe, some lancets and a saw, and a pamphlet on dissections. He would now be equipped with the tools of his new trade, and could look forward to working with Takesgun. Jack did not voice his misgivings aloud, but silently prayed that Stephen had not transmitted his coprophilia to the young lad.

Jack gave Stephen joy of his panther spoor, but was not to be delayed by his ship's surgeon. Dripping as he went, he stumbled back through the swamp, smacking at mosquitoes, yanking at leeches, glaring so furiously at the alligators that they backed away from his path, their yellow eyes glinting in the moonlight. Followed by his men carrying the gifts from his new friends and allies, he drooped noticeably as he gratefully boarded the dear *Aghast*. Stephen, trying out his newly acquired Southern patois, drawled "Howdy, y'all," as he was carried on board; if Jack was discouraged by Stephen's continued inability to tell a yawl from a frigate, he was too tired to correct him tonight. The men paired with their leeching partners, and provided Dr. Nattering with enough jarfuls of the useful creatures to last the entire voyage.

They watered at Barbados, the men sweating under the heavy barrels, but enjoying the sunshine and the feel of land beneath their feet nonetheless. Stephen explored the local flora, the men in shifts enjoying the fauna (bipedal, female), and all hands enjoyed tropical fruits before heading northward.

Back up the coast they sailed the next day; again seeing remarkably little marine traffic. Despite the careful search inflicted again upon Nattering upon his boarding the ship, Jack found it necessary to personally drop several snakes and lizards over the side of the ship, as they were startling his crew into error. If there were scorpions or tarantulas or yellowjack mosquitoes in Stephen's dunnage, as Jack believed likely, he had not the moral courage to search them out. It would not be the first nor the last time Stephen brought carriers of the bubbly brown tide aboardships.

Jack did not believe Stephen would have success with the Maryland farmers. Many of them were dissident with the central government, but he did not think they would betray it, although they would clearly not be averse to trade with the enemy. Stephen agreed with the assessment, and they decided that an attempt to recruit towards a rebellion might be counter-productive. The Florida gambit appeared prodigiously successful, but only time would tell. He believed the mission as a whole would therefore prove successful, and since Stephen had absolute discretion over the covert aspect of the mission, they decided that although Stephen would go ashore and reconnoitre the Maryland landscape, they would not push their luck if the situation appeared unpromising, especially since there was greater military than political need in the area for a British twenty-eight-gun, copper-bottomed frigate with a bluff bow and lovely lines. *Aghast* was only a sixth rate jackass frigate (five hundred seventy-nine tons) but the Maryland campaign was about to begin.

Jack told Stephen about the training vessel he had taken, and his meetings with Captain Hornbearer of the American navy. He told him confidentially about the business proposals Hornbearer had offered him; Stephen was more wary than Jack about land-based business deals that sounded too good to be true, but held his tongue—there would be time for considered advice when more information developed. Jack omitted from his account any mention of Mrs. Hornbearer or Katie, but Stephen had the confidence of the men of the ship, and fairly well knew the chain of events. They looked at the stars, the moon, the starlit sea. Gazing at the constellations, as familiar to him as his own hand, Jack started to explain to Stephen a few points about the science of navigation, but Stephen objected at the use of the word "science" in that context. Jack was surprised at that attitude.

"Well," he said patiently, "navigation is a very exacting science, I must say; we can't just go mucking about hacking off limbs the way a doctor does and hope to get from point A to point B—of course navigation is a science."

"Sure, and I hardly think that 'mucking about hacking off limbs' suffices to describe what a modern physician does," replied Stephen in an absurdly hurt tone. "Perhaps the original chirurgeons were less scientific than their followers..."

"Chirurgeons!" exclaimed Jack in amazement. "Is that where the term 'surgeon' comes from? From my observations of you, I thought, ha! Ha! Ha!..."

Stephen waited for it impatiently, drumming his fingers across his narrow chest.

Jack slapped his thigh hard enough to bruise, and laughed and laughed until tears streamed from his eyes.

Stephen usually enjoyed Jack's cheerful delight in his own supposed wit, but not when he had cause to believe that he himself would be the deflowered maiden[20].

"I thought... I thought..." But Jack could barely get the words out, until Stephen started to depart in a huff. "I surely thought," sputtered Jack, his vermilion face intensifying his sparkling blue eye, "That the word 'surgeon' derived from 'curmudgeon!'"

Stephen apparently was in an unreceptive mood for scientific discussion, because he excused himself and went off to bed, stuffing his ears with wax balls and dosing himself with one of the new herbal leaves he had harvested with Takesgun as an inducement to sleep. He had slept well for two weeks, and although he found the soothing sway of the hammock relaxing, he was morally certain that Jack had not learned to sleep quietly like a Christian during his absence.

Jack reported to Commodore Spring the next day, briefing him on *Aghast*'s availability but omitting details of Nattering's doings, and was assigned a support role to the small fleet assembling off the coast of Maryland.

---

[20] Stephen Nattering was actually more than a mere surgeon. He was developing a highly innovative theory of diseases and germes and treatments, following Jenner's case-studies with the most intense interest, and thought it likely that one day in the future, one could look forward to an announcement to the effect that "As to the diseases of the body, the physician is now in command. The microbiotiae which cause the acute infections are in full retreat. That retreat might before long become a rout."

17

Jack was sorry that he had missed Stephen's birthday, while Dr. Nattering had been in Florida. In retroactive celebration, he had Quillick prepare Stephen's favourite dessert, marchpan,[21] as well as his own favourite pudding, a floating archipelago in the shapes of Mrs. Williams, Sophie and Diana. To his surprise, both Doctor Stephen Nattering and Reverend Nathaniel Martinet got boisterously drunk at the birthday party, and both had to be carried out, singing together uncharacteristically loudly and very uncharacteristically merrily:

> Mures tres
> Mures tres
>
> Caeci currunt
> Caeci currunt

---

[21] Marchpan (mazapan, marzipan) (serves 6)

  3 cups almonds, blanched and ground
  2 cups granulated sugar
  1 cup water
  2 egg whites, beaten
  4 tbs powdered sugar
  1 tsp vanilla

Heat water and granulated sugar in saucepan until sugar is dissolved and mixture begins to boil. Let it boil steadily until the temperature reaches 230 degrees F on a candy thermometer, without stirring. Remove from heat and beat until mixture turns slightly cloudy.

Stir in ground almonds, egg whites and vanilla. Cook over gentle heat about 2 minutes, until mixture pulls away from the sides of the pan. Turn the mixture onto a surface that has been sprinkled with powdered sugar. Knead the mixture until smooth, working in the rest of the powdered sugar. Pull off pieces and shape into balls, and chill.

Sequuntur sponsam agricolae
Ab ea abscissae sunt caudulae
Est plenius nihil stultitiae

Quam mures tres
Mures tres.

The *Aghast* plied the waters of the Delmarva capes region, occasionally spotting a ship in the distance; however, the spring passed slowly, with very little action. Audibly was called aboard the *Cuchulainn* from time to time, to receive orders, or for dinner. He entertained Commodore Spring and his lieutenants, along with the officers of the rocketship *Erebus* and a Canadian vessel, regaling them with the local crab soup, crabcakes,[22] ruffed grouse with cameline sauce[23], lamb chops with a delightful sauce Stephen

---

[22] Maryland Crabcakes a la Quillick: (serves four, or Audibly and another)

  1 pound crabmeat, shells removed (1/14 stone)
  1 tsp salt
  1 tsp Old Bay seasoning
  1 tbs baking powder
  1 egg, beaten
  1 tbs Worcestershire sauce
  3 tbs mayonnaise
  1 tbs whole grain mustard
  2 ship's biscuits (two slices of white bread with crust removed may be
      substituted) Break into small pieces and moisten with milk.
  Oil for frying

1. Add salt, seasoning, baking powder, and biscuits to crabmeat, and stir.
2. Combine egg, Worcestershire sauce, mayonnaise, and mustard, then gently mix into crabmeat mix.
3. Shape into eight cakes and fry 2 to 4 minutes on each side.
NOTE: For crabcakes a la Audibly, add two pounds of scraps of whatever foodstuffs are available, ground to a mealy texture, before frying.

[23] Cameline Sauce
  Soak ship's biscuit or bread in vinegar and squeeze it out. Pound ginger, cloves, mace, and cinnamon together, and mix them with the bread. Salt to taste.

had devised as an antiscorbutic: although there was no danger of scurvy with the fresh fruits and vegetables available, the *Aghasts* and their guests all loved his "Catalan sauce,"[24] asparagus boiled to a fine paste, stewed apples, and a drowned baby and darioles for dessert. Maintaining a steady flow of discourse between chewing, Jack entertained them with his usual good humor. "As you know, there are three kinds of people in the Royal Navy: those who can count, those who can't..." He paused, his cheerful, weather-beaten face dropping. "I regret that I'm laid by the lee—I've forgotten the third kind."

"Don't worry, Jack," Stephen soothed. "I'm sure it will come to you with a touch more brandy."

Stephen enjoyed the *Schadenfreude* of Jack's momentary discomfiture, and cackling softly, continued to entertain. "Shall I tell you the two great secrets of success?" he asked.

Jack smiled happily. "Please do," he exclaimed, leaning forward to hear better.

"The first is, 'don't tell everything you know.'"

Jack waited, but as usual, Stephen's attention turned to other matters.

Jack regretted not having a deipnosophist at these dinners, but carried the conversation well enough with an occasional "A glass of wine with you, sir." From time to time during the course of the dinner he wrestled on the point of a tremendously witty remark, thought once that he'd achieved a half-Nelson on it, but never quite vanquished it. Rowan obliged them by reciting a new composition for them, about Audibly's most famous naval victory:

---

[24] Catalan Green Sauce: excellent on meats, even better on vegetables

  2-3 bunches fresh parsley, finely chopped
  8 tablespoons fresh garlic, finely chopped
  2 cups virgin olive oil
  1 cup white or balsamic vinegar

Combine all ingredients and let sit for three hours. Season to taste with salt and pepper. NOTE: This is also an excellent basting sauce for meats to be roasted.

Twas brailed up, and the sliding keel
Did gyre and gimbal in the wave;
All malmsey was the *Boreas'* wheel,
And the *Sophie* shot grape.

Beware the jackass rig, my son!
Le Guerrier, le Conquerant
Beware the *Cacafuego*, and shun
The frumenty and salmagundi at Ushant;
The gleet and pox at Port Mahon.

He pulled his voyol, and sword in hand
Long time the Manx shearwater he sought -
So rested he during the tramontan'
And stood a while in thought.

And as in offing thought he stood
The jackass rig, with tongues of flame
Came widdershins through the touchole hood
And bursten as it came!

One, two! One, two! And through the thread
The voyol-block went on the crossjack!
He left *Cacafuego* dead, and overturned its head
And went smoke-and-oakum back.

And has thou slain the *Cacafuego*, hey?
Come to my bed, you Benthamite boy!
Oh, figgy-dowdy day! We'll take Calais!
He chuckled in his joy.

'Twas brailed up, and the sliding keel
Did gyre and gimbal in the wave;
All malmsey was the *Boreas'* whcel,
And the *Sophie* shot grape.

154

Said Commodore Spring, "I've read nineteen books on the subject of naval battles, and this is the clearest exposition of a battle at sea I've encountered; in plainchant King's English."

Stephen noted with disapproval that Jack had gathered up all the saltcellars and biscuits, and was explaining to the captains with the greatest of lubricious cheer another recent battle: ". . . and my lieutenant was over here, do you see, with the lady's companion, and this was the placement of the musicians, and two of the chaperones lay thus..."

The dinner ended on a poor note, however; Doctor Nattering, responding to a call to visit the sick-berth, lost his balance when a froward wave lifted the *Aghast*, stumbling into Quillick bearing decanters of brandy and cups of sweetpudding—all guests were stained, Commodore Spring muttering under his breath something about a goddammed fat clumsy lobscouse, and the mood of the dinner was quite lowered. "Wittles is up, down, and all about," muttered Quillick under his breath. A lesser quality brandy was substituted, and Jack's embarrassment was evident as he bade his guests goodtide.

Stephen asked Jack about Rowan's recitation the next day, when Jack's headache had subsided.

"Sure, and I'm not the expert of the world on nautical terminology," he began.

Jack smiled benignly. "Is this going to be another 'Never mind, I'll ask Tom Pushings' sort of question? Ye'll not catch me at that again, I believe."

"Not at all, not at all," Stephen soothed. "But there was a word in the poem last night I did not quite catch the meaning of from the context."

Jack continued smiling. "I was confident that with your vast experience at sea you would have understood every word in the poem. Pray, what is troubling your comprehension? I would like nothing better than to clarify whatever is giving you difficulty."

Stephen nodded his head. "What did it mean when the line went 'did <u>gyre</u> and gimbal in the wave?' I'd not heard the word 'gyre' used that way."

Jack leaned back. "A 'gyre' is a tremendous wheel of water that makes a complete, clockwise turn in an ocean - such as the Gulf Stream in the Atlantic. The wind sets the water in motion, and the Earth's rotational forces twist the circulation into circular paths when this water bumps into the land masses we call 'continents.' The Gulf Stream acts like a river in the middle of the ocean."

"And does it affect the motion of the ship in any way?" Stephen asked, curiously.

"Indeed it does," Jack replied, startled at the question. "The Gulf Stream can carry a ship more than two hundred fifty miles a day! Were there any other parts of the poem you would like explained?"

Stephen thanked him, and went below to sort his bird specimens. He felt much better with the explanation, confident that he was now a more complete mariner, thoroughly knowledgeable in all aspects of naval life.

Some days passed, and although the watches were diligent, they saw no action at all. The American merchant vessels stayed out of sight of the English ships patrolling the coast. The small English fleet knew that the Colonists were slipping out unseen in small smuggling barks in the night, but they had too few ships, and were unable to find them. Jack morosely counted the prize money he was not winning, but nothing came within his range. He sat in the crosstrees with Stephen, sighing with a deep philosophical thought. Stephen dreaded Jack's philosophical thoughts, but fixed his face in an attentive mode, encouragingly.

"Have you ever wondered," Jack asked in a dreamy tone, "what your life would have been like had you been someone else?"

Stephen turned it over in his mind. He could not think of a single intelligent response, and sadly, gazing apologetically at his friend's eager face, he stuffed his ears with wax balls.

Something was definitely wrong on board the *Aghast*. Impossible as it seemed, Jack came on deck one morning and could have sworn that the mainmast was shorter than it had been the night before. The ship was springing strange leaks, and the hanging knees were weak, far weaker than they should have been. There were odd piles of sawdust here and there, and no-one could explain any of it. Men who were usually uncomplaining, such as Mr. Readey and Mr. Lackey, were suffering from implausible itches. Captain Audibly had midshipman Calumny summoned to his cabin.

"Mr. Calumny," he bellowed hoarsely in the youth's ear. "What the devil have you been up to?"

In the absence of a specific accusation to respond to, Calumny pleaded innocence. He had most definitely committed certain mischief over the past few days, as well as the previous few, but chose not to admit to any more than he had been red-handedly caught at.

"Speak up," Jack roared encouragingly. "You're soon to be an officer, God forbid, and it's a most serious offence ye've committed, and ye'll only make it harder on yourself by not coming clean!"

Calumny thought hard on what he might have been caught at, of his many gammons, and decided on one of the most obvious.

"Oh, sir!" he exclaimed piteously. "It's true I dropped a pig's bladder of blood on Mr. Williamson's head on deck from the foretopmast, but it made only a wee little splash, and the Doctor said I could have the blood from the sick-berth, in return for I had helped him hold down a few fo'c'slemen for his bleeding experiments, and the moppers cleaned it up ever so pretty..."

"What else, Mr. Calumny," Jack asked, in as reasonable and reassuring tone of voice as he could muster. His voice was so reasonable, in fact, that Calumny could easily count all the captain's teeth in his head, despite his serious mathematical limitations, and could also, with no difficulty at all, recite an accurate litany of everything Captain Audibly had eaten within the past several hours.

Calumny's eyes rolled in alarm in his head. "Well, sir," he replied trustingly, "perhaps I might have stuck some little frogs in the mids' hammocks, in truth. They stuck enormously well, with an application of portable soup to their legs; it's quite like glue, you would have loved to see it, I'm sure. And it did the frogs no harm, as they were able to feed well on the bugs that were attracted to the soup and got stuck in it themselves..."

Captain Audibly held his tongue, biding his peace.

"Upon my word, sir," Calumny went on, "it was not I who shortsheeted your cot. I'll not say who, on pain of death, I'll not peach on my mates in the midshipman's berth, but it was not I, nor Williamson nor Readey, nor Mr. Loki who done it, neither, on my word. Nor was it I who switched the salt and the sugar in the galley, and weren't Quillick the devil to pay!"

Audibly gazed at a spot slightly above Calumny's head, trying to control his eyes from rolling up in his head. He felt a serious sense of deja moo—he'd heard that line of bull before.

"Is it the water-bladder fights, sir? They are only meant in fun, sir,... as are the sugars in the mids' hammocks, and that didn't quite serve to attract the snakes, as I had expected, it was in vain, so to speak, but only in fun, sir."

Calumny heard the captain grinding his teeth, and panicked. He could not think of what else he had been actually caught at, having been most cautious in his endeavors, using all the guile and cunning he had learned in his five and ten in the Royal Navy. His blood froze at the thought of some actions, but reason prevailed; he could not have been caught out at his truly rotten-most pranks. Was he being unjustly accused of something he had not even done? He gazed earnestly into the Captain's eyes, and did not like what he there saw. Summoning all his courage, and gulping hard, he ventured one final desperate defense.

"Surely, surely, sir" he stammered, "you cannot conceive of pinning the rap on me for the loosening of the lids on the saltcellars, or the greasing of the handles of the bourguignonne—I had barely been breeched at that time, sir!"

Jack sent Calumny back. He had similarly polite discussions with all the other midshipmen, and elicited a prodigious aggregation of tomfoolery japes, boys will be boys, but nothing to explain the weak hanging knees, the sawdust, the very masts being rickety. Worse, he had the distinct impression that he had somehow laid himself by the lee with his best friend, because Stephen had not spoken three words to him in as many days, and refused to look him in the eye. He hoped Stephen was not working himself up to another duel; even though Stephen didn't know a portlast[25] from a portlid[26] from a potlid[27] from a pothead,[28] he was deadly with sword, pistol, numchucks, shillelagh, lancet, capsaicin-spiked purge-bag, bow and curare-tipped arrow, fisticuffs, tae kwon do, the barbed *mot*, and every other weapon known to Jack. On two earlier occasions Jack had been set up to duel with Nattering; he had averted disaster both times by pointing at pretended gillygaloos and whangdoodles behind the doctor, and sneaking away when Stephen turned in excitement to look, but he doubted his luck would hold a third time. He sent Baretta Blondin, with his compliments, to inquire as to the doctor's well-being, and should he care to step into the captain's cabin when convenient; and settled back to wait.

"And which he never sends compliments when he calls for me to do his bidding," whined Quillick at the door.

"Quillick! Blow it out your bleedin' _____ arse!" Jack roared without rising.

Some three pots of coffee and a small curried goat later, Stephen appeared, looking downcast and apprehensive. Jack drew him off guard by offering to share the remains of the goat. Stephen snuffled, and asked for Jack's friendship and good will; it would oblige him extremely. Audibly was, at this point, far too curious to hold out, and promised on his word that Stephen would not be flogged round the fleet, nor keelhauled, nor hanged, no matter what. A rash promise, he soon learned, but he manfully kept to it.

---

25 Portlast - a person from Maryborough, Ireland
26 Portlid - a small port
27 Potlid - the cover of a cooking vessel
28 Pothead - a derogatory term for a physician/surgeon who indulges in laudanum, the tincture of opium

"Sure, and you were a very good sport about the vampire bats," Stephen began. "I do indeed value a good sport, I prize it and your excellent tolerance and kindness above all your other best qualities; and you are the patient saint of all the world." Stephen was accustomed to Jack's resiliently cheerful countenance; as he spoke, the look of abject misery appearing on his friend's face stabbed at his heart.

After his initial dismay, Jack was thoroughly alarmed by Stephen's prolegomena. "Is it bees or wasps or hornets again?" he demanded. "Am I again to be denied access to my own sleeping cabin, as usual? Are there above a dozen poisonous rattlesnakes loose in my cabin?"

"Not at all, for all love!" Stephen shouted indignantly. "I am very well aware that you did not want me to bring bees and yellowjack mosquitoes on board the ship, and I always abide by your wishes, howsoever unreasonable they may be. You are, after all, the captain of the ship, are you not, and am I not your humble and obedient servant?"

Jack smiled amiably, although he had the strangest foreboding. It did not escape his keen mind that Stephen had denied bees and mosquitoes but had not responded on the rattlesnakes.

"Certainly not, by the saints," Stephen continued. "No bees. No wasps. Not a single solitary hornet." ("Again he failed to touch on snakes," Jack moaned to himself). Nattering started to depart, but Jack was catching wise to Stephen's tricks, and asked him with the softest and gentlest voice he could muster, "What were you about to say about the vampire bats and the good sport? Come, now, out with it, all at once, and you'll feel better for getting it off your puny chest."

Stephen looked about the cabin wildly, but saw no salvation on the walls or the planks. "I do hope you won't take this amiss," he gargled, "but by the most amazing stroke of bad fortune, a foul wave striking the vessel and heaving it all ahoo, and I must have accidentally left the glass lid off... and may I request Quillick to fetch you a double shot of brandy, because you are looking rather frail at the moment, and perhaps, perhaps we should really discuss this further another time..." He paused. "In case I should ever be stranded alone on a Royal Navy frigate," Stephen inquired, "should you care to instruct me now on the proper re-roving of the bowsprit gammoning? Puddening, I meant to say? Or would it be more useful in case of shipwreck if I were to learn to, as you say, flemish the falls, or priddy the maindeck?"

Jack's heart sank within him. He said nothing at all, but edged himself to block the door of the cabin, loosened his suddenly too-tight shirt-collar and crossed his immense forearms in front of his chest, and waited.

Stephen listened to the sounds of the wind in the rigging with great intensity.

Jack waited. Below the cabin, they could hear a ship's boy asking his mates in a plaintive voice had they seen his little nannygoat, Gertrude, anywhere, for he had left her feeding and now she was nowhere to be found. Stephen found he had not the moral courage to fix Jack with a stare; Jack, in turn, turned his attention to inspecting the manicure Quillick had given him that morning— he thoroughly detested ragged fingernails.

Jack noticed that Stephen was not saying anything, a most unusual state for Stephen. "Yes," he prompted, "what exactly was in the cage that you left the glass lid off when the ocean decided to cast a wave in the middle of the sea where no Christian could possibly expect a wave to rise?"

Stephen swallowed hard, and whispered something in Catalan.

"In English, please," Jack reminded him.

"*Rhinotermitidae*," Stephen mumbled. "*Reticulitermes flavipes*, to be exact. Of the order *Isoptera*, of course. May I be excused now? I believe the catharpins are singing in the larboard keels."

Jack continued to block the door bodily. He thought for a while, replaying the words in his head, conjugating, parsing furiously. "D'ye mean to tell me...?" he began.

Stephen nodded, grinning. "Ain't it prime?" he asked, relieved that the ordeal was over.

Jack thought about it, light slowly dawning, trying his best to block out the light that dawned, but unsuccessfully blocking it. His head hurt, and cold sweat dribbled down his back. "D'ye mean to tell me... that you brought termites onto the *Aghast*?" he asked sweetly.

"Oh, Jack, my love, I'm so glad you understand!" Stephen sighed with relief.

Jack dared not risk turning Stephen sullen at this juncture—he had to have information, or his ship would founder. "Might I be permitted to ask," Jack smiled through the blood in his eyes, "how many termites we might be talking about?"

Stephen grew concerned. Jack's mouth was smiling, but his ears were beginning to bleed, and a very unhealthy vein was about to pop in his forehead, a calenture lurking nearby was not vastly unlikely; and although Jack would certainly benefit from being bled a pint or two, Stephen did not think this was a good time to broach the issue.

"By the saints," he murmured, "*ne quid nimis* - I only brought on less than a dozen, but as you probably know, the female queen can produce some thirty thousand eggs a day. But!" he exclaimed, seeing Jack's face take on an unhealthy tinge, "but these are the loveliest specimens you could ever hope to see. If you're to have termites loose on a king's ship, of the two thousand species of the world, the *rhinotermitidae* are the most beautiful by far. Oooh, the fontanelles on the adults; the four-segmented tarsi! And would you believe that the scale of the forward wing is longer than the pronotum? They even have a nasuti caste, with heads drawn out anteriorly into their snouts, for better defense of the colony. Surely you see the benefit to mankind from the princely termite family - where would our ecology devolve to if termites failed to convert dead trees into more useful substances to plants and animals alike, I ask you?"

Jack seemed more donnered than Stephen had ever seen him.

"Thirty thousand eggs a day?" he repeated dumbly. "The Irish! And do they live a great many days?"

Stephen beamed happily. "Sure, and the queen can cheerfully go on for thirty years or more, and in good health. When she gets into her reproductive stride, given ample nutrition, which I expect to provide (there being no shortage of termite nutrition on board the *Aghast*, praise the saints), her abdomen can enlarge from the termite norm of a centimeter to as much as eleven centimeters long, would you believe the joy of it all?"

They heard a voice calling "Here, Gertrude, my pretty Gertrude, here girl!" followed by a series of falsetto bleats, whinnies, and moos from the riggings and topmasts. Jack bellowed out without moving for the lieutenant to take the names of the midshipmen who were so braying.

Stephen paused. It was clear to him that Audibly was going to be unreasonable about this, as he had been unreasonable about so many important scientific experiments. In vain did he explain that this colony would soon die out of natural causes; *Reticulitermes flavipes*, a subterranean species of termites, required moist soil to live in; did Jack think he was so unthinking, so foolish, so inconsiderate as to bring *Kalotermitidae*, the damp- wood termites, onto the ship? Or *Coptotermes havilandi*, a quite destructive beast Stephen would never intentionally inflict on a ship, could Captain Audibly credit him with that?

But: *si finis bonus est, totum erit*. Jack desired Stephen to rid the ship of every last one of the varmints, and reluctantly, Stephen went ashore and borrowed a honey bear from a priest he knew to keep such as pets. He did exact a promise from Audibly not to eat the bear, a promise eagerly granted, and a few days later, the fat and contented honey bear was returned safely to his owner, and the masts stopped shrinking, the hanging knees, although unable to heal themselves, at least stopped their weakening, and the sawdust swept away by the sweepers did not return. Jack resumed his normal affability, and Stephen was once again in good graces, and was even granted leave to go ashore the next day, the men of the *Aghast* being in extraordinary good health as a result of the fresh produce coming in daily, courtesy of the cheerfully entrepreneurial American greengrocers; and suffering from nothing more serious than a few cases of the strong fives and the usual bear-bites, bee-stings, and snake-bites that Dr. Nattering had always found to be routinely prevalent on every royal naval ship he had ever sailed on. He agreed to submit to a strip-search of his bodily cavities upon his return, and retired to play the nightly round of music with the captain.

As soon as they began tuning their instruments, a plaintive wail arose from the deck—"Is that you, Gertrude?"

The days grew milder; soft spring zephyrs with breath favonian favoured the *Aghast*'s captain, doctor, and men alike, and the night skies waxed their fulgence as the frigate wore on and off, day and night after day and night.

18

Stephen Nattering loved everything he saw in Maryland. From aboard *Aghast*, he saw flounder, that remarkable flatfish. He knew, but had never before observed, that when flounder hatch from the egg as tiny fry, they swim upright in the water, just as other fishes do. When they are still quite small, however, they sink to the bottom of the water and lie on one side. The upper side takes on the colour of the bottom, and the lower side becomes white. The lower eye crosses over to the upper side of the fish, so that grown flounders have both eyes on the same side. Stephen was amazed to see them thus.

Ashore, he spotted timber wolves, black bears with the most delightfully pungent spoor, from which he extracted whole bottlefuls of fimicolous creatures; an elk, woodland bison, all sorts of deer and rabbits, and a wonderful muskrat. He was utterly entranced by the whooping cranes (*grus americanus*) and their eerie courtship dance, with its bowing, bobbing, leaping, weaving, jumping, wing-flapping; its call could be heard from two miles distance! It was so white that it glowed against the clouds; so large that its flight appeared to be a study in slow motion. It was nearly as large as he was; fully five feet tall, and weighed nearly sixteen pounds. He dissected one, with barely controlled enthusiasm, to determine the source of its trumpet, and was amazed at its trachea, which was over five feet long. He retrieved from within the crane, among other things, three sovereigns, and a ring numbered T.S. 206. He pondered it for a while; wondering what he would find if he dissected Captain Audibly - would a hyperextended five-foot trachea account for the sonic buffet of his nocturnal emission? How different the *Gruinae* crane was from *Balearicinae* he had dissected in Africa, the Crowned Crane, which had straight trachea (they honked rather than whooped!), colourful facial markings, and elaborate crests! "Sure," he muttered to himself as he cut, "and man has been interfering with cranes since the thirteenth century, when Marco Polo described the phasianids in the gardens of Kublai Khan. Cutting up one or two more won't signify." He was immensely pleased with the bird, despite its having slashed him cruelly upon its capture with its razor-sharp middle toe. Perhaps its most endearing trait was its ability to sleep standing up, as so many cranes do, balanced on one leg in eight inches of water. This simple defense protects the sleeping cranes from bobcats, which can't sneak up on the birds without splashing. (The African Crowned Cranes, on the other hand, faced different predators; so they roosted in trees)! The whooping crane's trachea fascinated him, as it coiled within, fusing with the sternum so that the trachea and sternum actually amplified the calls produced in the larynx of the bird.

The different types of crane callings also interested Stephen, from the low, purr-like contact calls, the slightly louder pre-flight calls, the shrill pre-copulatory calls, the groan-like distress calls, the screaming location calls, the abrupt alarm calls, the loud flight calls and guard calls, but especially, he enjoyed the loud, complex duets of the unison calls, in which the male emits a long series of low calls, and the female accompanies him with two or three high-pitched calls for each call of the male.

He also enjoyed seeing the flowers of the Maryland countryside: Laylocks, syringas, hyacinths and particularly roses: Burgundy rose plants, a cluster rose, a Hundred leaf rose, moss roses and rose *de Meaux.*

He lit a small fire and roasted mushrooms for his lunch; wild morels, with the erotic, mysterious savour of an older woman's armpit filling his nostrils and his inner mind.

He walked up into the mountains one day. His heroes, Cuvier and LaMarck, had both talked of using fossils to show how extinct animals might have looked, although neither had developed their theories much as yet; Cuvier was concentrating on animals with backbones, and LaMarck talked about his intention to study fossils of shellfish and worms. Stephen wanted to explore the fossils of the Appalachians, to see if they were different from the fossils he had found in European mountains and in Chile, and to see if he could find any specimens of interest, either for himself and Banks or to pass along to more knowledgeable explorers. Geology was a fairly undeveloped science, and there was hope of new discoveries and theories, although it was obvious that very little could ever be learned from studying rocks. Probably, geology would never be a true science, having little to do with the real world, despite a passing curiosity by genuine scientists. Recently, the Scotsman James Hutton had differentiated classes of rocks, and had proposed the theory that the earth"s crust is the result of structural changes still in progress, but probably the greatest explorer of geology of all time was the famous naturalist Compte de Buffon, who believed that geological history was displayed as a series of stages, and that the earth may have originated as a fragment of the sun, pulled off by a passing comet. Buffon had established his credentials as a scientist by showing how a boiled infusion of meat would teem with bacteria after standing in a closed container for a few days, proving conclusively that bacteria arose spontaneously. However, he had unfortunately stated that the planet earth was more than seventy thousand years old; a preposterous claim without any substantial backing. Perhaps Buffon should have stuck to translations of the works of others. Unhappily, his brilliant son, who had traveled as a companion to Lamarck, would not be around to further his father's work—the Mob had seen to that. Even the former American president, Thomas Jefferson, had made notable contributions to the field, with his archeological excavations and his fossil collections; yet Stephen was dismayed at the lack of concrete information about the structural foundation of the planet. In the Appalachians of Maryland, he found samples of both igneous and metamorphic rocks, and oddly, some of the same species of sea fossils that had been found in the Alps. Was this due to simultaneous Creation of both chains, or had some natural force caused sea creatures to be lifted to the heights of the tallest mountains he had ever encountered? He was not what Hutton would term a "geologist," but to his practiced naturalist's eye, it would have taken more than a mere forty days and nights of flooding, even with a year of subsidence, to lay those fossil beds in the mountains. He loaded up two midshipmen with rock samples, and happily scampered back to the *Aghast.*

He attempted to share his discoveries and theories at dinner the next afternoon. "Subduction begets orogeny," he warbled cheerily. Jack stared at him, casting a sidelong glance at Reverend Martinet.

"Doctor, recall yourself!" he urged. Stephen smiled blissfully, happily, as Nathaniel Martinet looked away in embarrassment.

All in all, he had some most delightful days, and they were only part of a series of delightful days in Maryland. Once, when *Aghast* was anchored in a sheltered cove, hoping for some American shipping interests to put out, he was gazing at the dawning sun from his crosstrees. A bird flew over, its feathers glowing pink from the rising sun; as he strained to identify it in the glare of the sun, it was followed by another, and then a dozen, a hundred more, and a flock of billions of passenger pigeons (*ectopistes migratorius*) blotted out the sun for three days. "Bird," said Audibly. "Bird... bird... bird-bird-bird." Baretta Blondin was kind enough to net some for the doctor. The male had grey upper parts, with black wingtips and tail; its throat a dark rust, whilst its breast was a lighter shade of rust; even its eyes were red. The female was of a duller colour, of course, with brownish upper parts and a lighter brown throat and breast; the female's eyes were black. The young resembled the females, but the tips of their head, neck, and upper breast feathers had white tips. Their dung fell to the deck like blankets of snow for three days; Captain Audibly and all hands aboard grew heartily sick of Stephen giving them joy every time a bird befouled them. Quillick had to wrap Stephen's new green sweater around the Captain's epaulettes to protect them; he knew the doctor wouldn't mind at all. Stephen was amazed that the Philistines of the crew were not as amazed nor as full of admiration for the flight as he was. Stephen wondered, dreamingly, of the outcome should a flock of passenger pigeons encounter a swarm of locusts. He knew that a locust swarm could be over thirty miles long, five miles wide, and could easily contain five hundred billion locusts, the swarm weighing a hundred thousand tons. For destructive power, a swarm of locusts would daily eat as much food as twenty million people. God preserve the passenger pigeons, Stephen thought to himself. He watched in awe, never sleeping, barely eating, for three full days as they passed overhead, without a break in the darkness or the droppings, ("bird-bird-bird-bird" muttered Jack) and Stephen slowly contrived a scheme for the betterment of the Royal Navy - if nets could be shot from a cannon, or even simply hoisted by balloons, they could trap enough of the birds to feed the Royal Navy for years to come - the supply of passenger pigeons was endless, infinite. He presented his scheme one evening to Jack Audibly, in a brief paper - *On the Improved Feeding of the Royal Navy: A Modest Proposal, by Doctor Stephen Nattering, Esqr., MD, RN,* but Audibly, not unexpectedly, rejected it out of hand. The man seemed to have no sense whatsoever that the Navy could be improved on in any way whatsoever.

"They wouldn't eat it, you know," he had explained gently, patiently to Stephen, in the manner of one explaining to a child why sweets could not be eaten in lieu of dinner. "They prefer their tack, weevilly though it be, and their salt beef and pease porridge and their holy salt pork days. I agree that a bird in the mouth is worth two in the hand, but squabs would be sorely wasted on them."

"But surely," Stephen pleaded, "for the good of the navy..."

"Good it may be," replied Jack. "If you insist, you may send your paper to the Office of Redundancy Office, but it simply would never do. Take care how you present yourself—you don't want to be arsing around with the old ways of the navy, like a Frenchman. If Admiral Tarte was to hear you, I daresay he would turn you adrift on a plank with your nether parts nailed to it, too, to teach you not to monkey with the men's rations, which they work hearty for and deserve hearty. Pigeon pie, indeed!"

Jack briefly considered Stephen's scheme for his own pantry, but dismissed it. He'd shot a few passenger pigeons for sport during his own days ashore in the colonies, but although they were excellent in pies,[29] there simply wasn't enough meat on them to fill him. Stephen wisely refrained from mentioning the *grus americanus*. For Captain Audibly, as for the rest of brute creation, there were only three kinds of birds; the delicious (which class included the vast majority of birds by far), the edible (which included most of the remaining birds, except those that had been dead and decayed over a fortnight), and the fantastical.

Ashore, alone, Stephen had the leisure to pursue his own thoughts, resolve whatever problems troubled his mind which could not be resolved on board ship with Audibly muttering constantly in his ear about cross-catharpings and tehuantepecs and langridges. Stephen doubted that such words even existed—he sometimes believed Audibly to be mispronouncing something else, deblaterating, or making up syllables to suit his needs, with the other officers simply humouring their captain by accepting the preposterous sounds; while Jack himself denied other men their pet phrases, even going so far as to express bewilderment at the common expression "flying by the seat of his pants." Now, under a clear, nearly cloudless sky with a warm breeze blowing, he indulged himself on a hilltop in visualizations. He could close his eyes, and an image would appear to him—sometimes a patch of color, sometimes a scene such as a wood or meadow, sometimes a surprising object. He would describe whatever it was aloud,

---

[29] Passenger Pigeon Pie (serves eight)

Debone four and twenty passenger pigeons, except the legbones, and marinate them for forty-eight hours in brandy, madeira, salt, pepper, and spices.

Dice a pound of boned pork and eight ounces fatback, brown in lard, and then chill. When cold, pound in a mortar, adding a half dozen truffles. Force through a sieve.

Reshape the passenger pigeons, and stuff with the pork forcemeat, a piece of truffle, and a piece of foie gras.

Line a piepan with flaky piecrust, cover the bottom with bacon, top with pork forcemeat, and lay the passenger pigeons on top, with forcemeat and truffle pieces between the birds. Top with another layer of piecrust, and dot with butter. Bake at 250F for 1 1/2 hours.

always aloud, as to an imaginary companion. As he described it, in the most infinitesimal detail, the image would change, and as it changed, he would describe the evolving image in rich, sensory-laden detail. As the image continued to evolve, it more often than not would turn into some surprising scene or image or detail that would provide a clue to a problem his mind was troubling with. He knew that this process of problem-solving was not unique to him—everyone he had confided his visualization to could learn to do it for themselves, to solve their own problems which were so different from his own, the Dear One knows, so very different, but the technique worked amazingly well.

Dr. Nattering believed that the mind works on the problems at a subconscious level; but as one concentrates on a problem, either it is resolved or it is not. If it is not resolved by thought, then further thought simply rehashes and reinforces the unfruitful solutions, and drives from consciousness any alternative solutions. The imaging technique allows the brain to catch hold of the fleeting glimpses of solutions that the brain produces but the conscious mind rejects. He wondered why that happened that way.

Perhaps, he thought, it is because we so much stress attentiveness to concrete thoughts, that we train ourselves to reject the images that surely are with every child in the world, until such time as he is educated, and taught to sit up straight and pay attention to what is being said by the tutor instead of what is being imaged within his own mind. When we internalize the instructions that we receive so vehemently and absolutely, we learn to ignore our own solutions to our own problems, and to focus only on the information presented to us externally. Most people Stephen had met in his professional career had so strongly internalized the "pay attention" instruction that they were even unaware of their own images. A little practice usually brought it back, however, opening to the practitioner a whole new world of problem-solving abilities.

Access to land was no problem for any of the men. Coastal security was poor, and the fact that the Englishmen physically resembled so many of the Americans, and the common language, made passage ridiculously simple. Dialect differences could be attributed to regional variations, and the population in Maryland towns was large enough that strangers did not unduly arouse suspicion, as long as they didn't order their bitters by the pint. Even the midshipmen had no difficulty in rowing ashore and stocking their meagre larders with pilfered poultry. Captain Audibly disapproved of the practice, of course, but that did not stay him from accepting half the proceeds of their nocturnal raids for his own table. Mr. Blabbington snuck quietly aboard the ship on many a night with a palm and four fingered impress on his otherwise flushed face. Dr. Nattering recognized the signs, and began preparing Blabbington's doses. When next he saw the lad preparing to slip ashore, he asked in as nasty a tone as he could muster, "Mr. Blabbington, should you like your hammock sent ashore?"

"Oh, yes, doctor, that would be the greatest kindness!" replied Blabbington, grinning like an ape as he climbed down the side.

"Sure, and Priapus ain't in it," Nattering muttered to himself. Blabbington and the midshipmen always referred to his upcoming infirmity as "the French disease;" Mr. Pompideau, bosun's mate, called the same symptoms "the English disease;" it was called "the Italian disease" by the Scots aboard the ship, and "the Indian disease" by most of the other Europeans; none that Stephen knew of called it anything but a Christian disease, (although Molly Tarte had once referred to it as "sailors' eyes"), and he sighed as he counted out his supply of blue pills. He had noticed similar nationalistic euphemisms for other deeds, of course; bestiality was termed "the Italian vice" by Spanish and Catalans of his acquaintance; homosexuality was universally known as "the Greek way," and paederasty itself was frequently dubbed "the English missionary position." He sighed again, and recounted.

Jack and Stephen went riding one mild day. The boys had procured a pair of horses; an oversized stallion for Jack, its flanks gleaming in the sunlight, and a lovely filly with a long, gracefully curved neck for Stephen, who fell in love with the horse at first sight, and named her 'Mona.' He reflected, as he rode through the gorgeous countryside, on the name. He had had several beasts named Mona—the name he assigned to all members of various species that distinguished themselves by graceful, elegant necks, or arrow-erect carriages, or delicately curved ears, or auburn coloration of a shade—each had died mysteriously, showing symptoms of poisoning; but Diana denied knowledge, and he believed her, of course, but it left him puzzled. He could not in good faith pin the rap on Jack Audibly, who had been at some great distance away on a few of the occasions. Mr. Calumny was quite proud of Captain Audibly's horse, wrapping his arms around its withers and thumping its broad chest happily.

"Ain't it a prime animal," he shouted, and Jack had to admit that it was prime indeed, with its brown eyes shining fiercely at the anticipated gallop.

This was not the first time they had ridden in Maryland. A few days earlier, the boys had gotten them a pair of long-eared *equus asinus* beasts. They had ambled about at a leisurely pace, savouring the weather, nipping at a keg of rum. Jack had thought to spark the animals to greater speed by feagueing their fundaments with ginger. The animals brayed piteously; Stephen, running back from his botanizing in alarm at the sound, instantly smoked the deed, and cried reproachingly, "Jack, you have quite debauched my ass!"

On the horse, however, Jack rode well, although the horse did not care to jump, as normal British horses would do, and they therefore had to circumnavigate obstacles; a nuisance, to his mind. Stephen's mind was still taken up with constupration, and he watched Jack's posture on the horse suspiciously. Jack sat well on a horse. The horse wobbled under his weight on occasion, but had good heart, and nickered winningly at Stephen for lumps of sugar. Stephen pointed out a magnificent oak tree in fine spring fettle. The mighty arms spread aloft and alow, but the small leaves made it seem cute, almost coy. Jack glanced at it, categorized his observation in his mind—"a tree"—and rode on. He stopped after a few yards and circled back, his mind calculating board-feet and comparing his observations with termite damage. He would send Blondin back later to impress the tree for the good of the Royal Navy. Stephen attempted to make conversation as they rode, marveling aloud that it is only horses and humans that have hymens, but Jack cut the conversation short by assuring Stephen that his stallion most assuredly did not; Stephen did not take kindly to being corrected on a matter of animal physiology; he was speaking of the species, not an individual. Their discussion turned to a happier note as they stopped at a tavern and enjoyed a splendid lunch. Stephen prattled happily about the Allegheny mountain chain in Maryland, part of the Appalachian mountains.

"Shall I tell you how the Appalachians got their name?" he inquired, with a cheery grin?

Jack was pleased that Stephen was in a good mood, making small jokes, and readily encouraged him.

"A Frenchman saw the mountains, and named them, and the appellation (Appalachian) stuck!"

Jack thought about it for a while, studied Stephen's unusually merry face, and slowly, very slowly, dissolved into belly-heaving mirth.

"Shall I order wine?" Jack asked.

"Owing to the warmth of the day and the joy of the ride," Stephen smiled, "I believe I'd prefer to drink ale or beer, well and perfectly brewed and cleansed and settled and defecate."

Jack stared at him, amazed, but Stephen smiled back, amiably, sardonically. Jack was weak, not having eaten for over an hour, and he outdid himself enormously in his consumption of hasenpfeffer and roasted potatoes. Jack Audibly never appeared to be eating much; indeed, he kept up a steady flow of amiable conversation, and seemed to be toying with his food, and yet, huge quantities of food disappeared in a remarkably short time. Stephen was reminded of the anaconda snake—it engulfed a week's worth of food in a gulp, and then digested it at its leisure. Jack Audibly did the same for the first half, but did so at every meal and opportunity. When they came back out, the horse accepted an apple eagerly, brushing his head against Jack's chest as he ate it; however, as soon as they mounted, the horse sighed deeply, sank to its knees, its eyes glazed over, and it emitted a curious sound as its last breath expired.

It was a long walk back, leading Stephen on his little filly, and Stephen stubbornly refused to rotate turns. Poor Captain Audibly was in such a snit when they returned to *Aghast* that Stephen of his own accord released the skunk he'd brought back in a little gunny sack, and boarded the ship without a slip or a comment. This was more painful for Stephen than he could have explained. He was familiar with other members of the *mustelid* family, but the New World skunk was quite different from the weasels, badgers, and otters he had known. He had hoped to dissect this small specimen and determine if it properly fit into the *mustelid* family at all; but it obviously was not to be. Jack watched the skunk with narrowed eyes as Stephen was hoisted aboard the *Aghast*. It glared at him with equally narrowed eyes, and raised its tail. Jack backed away. The skunk hissed at him, and arched its back, demurely stamping its little black paws. Jack retreated with a speed and grace unexpected for a man of his size and configuration.

As Captain Audibly boarded the *Aghast* (on the larboard side) and stripped off his uniform, a tear welled, glistened briefly in Quillick's eye, rolled down his broad cheek, moistening his beard, and dripped silently to the freshly holystoned deck.

19

The war went slowly. There was little traffic; they wore to and fro, patrolling their sector as long as there was light to see by; fishing was good, and the entrepreneurial Marylanders plied them with livestock, produce, textiles, tobacco, and occasionally, female companionship.

Stephen shot awake in the middle of a restless night, a roaring noise in his ears. "The French fleet is out!" he shouted, three parts awake. "The main battle has begun! I must get my instruments—go to my station—God between us and evil." Jack rolled over heavily, drowsily noting Stephen's alarm. "I wasn't snoring, was I?" he asked hoarsely. "I hope I didn't wake you out of your dream." Stephen sighed. Jack was starting to pull on trousers, although it was hardly a few half-bells in the morning. There would be no further sleep—Jack was rattling around as usual, eager to face the dawn, eager for Stephen to see something or other that would surely still be there at a more Christian hour. "I don't know why we have to turn out even before the cock croaks," he murmured in vain, scratching between his toes in the semi-dark.

Jack and Stephen sat one day in the masts, each lost in his own reveries, listening to the breezes, gazing at the sky and sea, but in greatly differing proportions. "What did you think on, just then?" Stephen asked suddenly.

"Nothing," Jack replied. "I wasn't thinking of anything at all."

"Forsooth, you were too, indeed," Stephen insisted. "I saw you catch your breath as something occurred to you."

"And now your physician skills allow you to tell me what I was thinking of, and I tell you I wasn't thinking of anything, and you can deny it?" Jack asked mildly.

"Not <u>what</u> you were thinking of, merely <u>that</u> you were a'thinking it," Stephen replied. "You see, as your mind catches onto something, you reflexively hold your breath while you are struck by it. Everyone does it, and no-one seems to be aware of it."[30]

Jack thought. "Actually," he muttered, "I was thinking of Sophie's sweet face, but atop... someone else's body, but it didn't warrant mention."

Stephen watched him closely. "Aha!" he exclaimed. "You were thinking of something again! You caught your breath as you attended to the thought!"

"So, what of it," Jack asked peevishly. "If everyone does it, what does it signify? If you could read my thoughts, it would be a better matter."

"Let me explain. If this observation of mine holds, then there is much more to be learned. It seems to me obvious that events shape our breathing patterns. We hold our breath at the first sign of danger, but why? It would be more pro-survival if we would suck in a great lungful, to prepare ourselves for fight or flight; but instead we stop breathing for an instant. I have myself noticed how some weak, simpering women catch their breath upon gazing upon a handsome male face (stop that flushing, I did not mention you by name, nor could any rational being consider your face anything more than interesting, I am sorry to enlighten you!) And men, too, alter their breathing patterns when a female shape floats by. Since the two elements, breathing and awareness, interact, I wonder if it is possible that our breathing also shapes our events, our motions, our actions. Possibly, if we could extend our breathing capacity, we could think more clearly, act more definitively, even extend our thought process; for surely, we formulate our thoughts in words; if we were capable of expressing more words in a breath, we could think a more complete thought, instead of breaking it into breath-sized phrases, with other, less meaningful phrases interspersed in just when we least can afford the interruption, when our thought is not fully formed... Do you find it at all interesting to speculate upon?"

---

[30]   Ed. note to Reader: Were you holding your breath as you read that sentence?

"Look, Stephen!" interjected Jack. "Look at that dark cloud forming up yonder. I don't doubt we'll have squalls shortly."

"Please attend a moment," Stephen begged. "It is of prime importance to me, and I value your opinion greatly, all the more because your perspective is so different from mine."

Jack squinted at him. As a naval captain, he was unaccustomed to being called to attention; but his affection for Stephen and his respect for Stephen's insights overrode his pique, and his natural curiosity was aroused by the doctor's eager intensity as he wrestled with the concept, even to the point of ignoring the louse crawling down Stephen's neck.

"Much as I hate to feed your grossly overblown opinion of yourself, I have to admit," Stephen continued, "that your musical abilities have much improved over the past years. Might it possibly be a result of your habit of swimming under the sea as much as you do? The practice surely improves your breath capacity; possibly as your breathing capacity increases, your ability to grasp larger phrases of musical passages improves in direct correspondence— you can play longer segments as a unity, in proportion to your unified awareness over a longer span of time. It is the same with thought—the longer your breath span, the fewer the interruptions to your thought processes as you formulate or digest new ideas, and the better, therefore, your understanding. I am not blind to the great improvements you have made in both your interest and your understanding of mathematics, physics, and astronomy over the time you have been engaged in the breath-building activity of swimming, and especially the underwater variety of swimming."

"Please continue," Jack said gravely. He was, by now, fully engaged in the doctor's explanation.

"When upset, or overcome by an undesirable, seemingly uncontrolled emotion" Stephen expounded, "I find that deliberate attention to my breathing pattern can effect alterations in my very feelings. Some people count to ten when upset; I control my breathing instead, and find that it works wonders. Have you experienced anything like that in yourself?"

Jack had to admit that as a captain, he was seldom required to control his emotions on the ship—he could rant and rave to his heart's content, and everyone within reach would knuckle their foreheads and say "Aye, sir." However, it would be helpful to gain control of his feelings when faced with an untoward admiral, court board, or bureaucrat. Further, he sometimes wondered if the men would respond better in crisis if he could contain his bellowing somewhat, although he had no intention of doing so merely to soothe their hurt feelings; crewmen required a certain handling if discipline were to be maintained on a warship, this wasn't a goddammed cruise ship to the East Indies, after all.

"How exactly do you control your breathing?" he asked out of curiosity.

"For one, I practice, especially when I am not under immediate stress, so that I can gain the pattern in comfort, and have it ingrained in me when I need it. For control of anger, upset, or even pain, I slow my breathing rhythm, taking four or five really deep, as deep and slow as I can make them, deep breaths, and then, as I continue in this rhythm, I imagine myself to be sucking my inhalations from the bottoms of my feet, and pulling the air all through my body. As I suck it up, I pretend that the air is attracting to itself, and dragging up, all my tensions, pains, and anger, and then as I exhale forcefully, I imagine myself to be blowing out the feelings I wish to dispel. Just two to three minutes of this pattern allows me to dispel anger and pain, and to deal rationally with the situation at hand."

"I see," said Jack, wondering to himself if this could really work, or if Stephen was under the influence of some narcotic even as he spoke. He relished the image of Stephen Nattering sucking his breath up from the soles of his feet, and wondered at the smell of such breath—Stephen had never been known to wash his feet other than by falling into the sea at inopportune moments.

"You may recall that I have found it necessary from time to time to perform surgical operations on myself. To dislodge

Canning's bullet from my chest, for example. I am as susceptible to pain as any other human, but I dare not allow anodyne, which might cloud my judgment or dull my skills. My only relief at such times is my breathing, and forsooth, the technique I have just described to you alleviates the mind and body of much pain." Stephen paused at this time, and breathed quite deliberately, to dispel the anxiety that the remembered episode caused him.

"For my enjoyment, and to imbue myself with the most delightful mood, I deliberately slow my breathing rhythm as before, but now I let my breaths out in the longest, most prolonged, most pleasurable sigh I can muster. I take great pleasure in doing so. I then imagine myself to be smelling a most pleasant scent, such as that of my wife's neck, or the scent of vanilla. When possible, I reinforce the practice by actually using my wife's neck or a source of vanilla in practice; however, imaginary practice also works."

Jack's attention wandered, as he considered the delightful scent of Diana's neck. He snapped back, replaying Stephen's last few sentences which he had not heard directly when lost in daydream. Had Stephen divined the reason for his piratical grin at the mention of Diana's neck; was that why he was scowling?

"I also find," said Stephen with some annoyance (obviously not exercising his breathing control), "that I can imagine myself to be stroking a strip of soft, smooth velvet, and I try to imagine myself breathing the luscious feel of velvet."

"I can't say that I even recall what velvet smells like," Jack remarked.

"It's not the smell, but the sensation, the comparison in your mind's eye. What if your breath were as smooth and as supple as velvet? That's the sensation I try to acquire. Or else, I imagine my breath to be stroking me, as if I were that strip of velvet. When my breathing pattern is velvety smooth, I find myself in a better cast of mood; I enjoy my food more, I sleep better. If I practice velvety-patterned breathing as I go to sleep, I sleep very well, and awaken much refreshed."

They sat for a while, trying out the experience together; Stephen was puffing out his aggravation with Jack's blatant reaction to the mention of Diana; Jack was grinning his most annoyingly robust, erotic grin as he imagined clearly and distinctly the remembered smell of Diana's neck.

"Shall we try a variation on the exercise?" Stephen inquired, in a perfectly calm state of equanimity.

"It certainly looks like a squall," Jack responded calmly and very happily, and shot down to the deck to have the preventer-stays rigged.

Two of the midshipmen, on a rare day of shore liberty, had met up with some American boys their age, and had sported about in a rather undignified manner, playing a form of cricket that seemingly had no rules; they had dined well in the boys' home, and had then gone on a snipe hunt; unfortunately, the American boys who were to drive the snipes had apparently lost their way in the dark, being totally ignorant of stellar navigation, and nothing was caught. The boys returned to the ship with a bad case of sniffles, and after deticking them, Dr. Nattering gave them a dose of chamomile tea laced with assafoetida, and made them forego meat for two days.

Jack asked Stephen about the use of rockets—he had never used them before himself, but knew they were coming increasingly into play, and were planned for the upcoming assault.

"Sure, rockets had been used in warfare for hundreds of years," Stephen began pedantically. He loved to demonstrate his superior knowledge to his friend, who never failed to come it high when he knew some trivia about seamanship that would be of no earthly use to anyone at all on land, man's natural habitat. "When the Mongols laid siege to K'ai-feng, that noble capital of Hunan province, the Chinese defenders had used a form of rockets to defend the city, shooting 'arrows of flying fire,' as far back as 1232. During the same battle, the defenders also dropped from the walls of the city a kind of bomb described as 'heaven-shaking thunder,' which was another form of rocket. The gunpowder the Chinese had developed was thus used both for propulsive rockets and for a form of explosive bombs. The Mongols themselves then exported rocket technology to Europe, in the Battle of Legnica in 1241."

Jack listened attentively. He hoped Stephen would soon get to the good stuff—the modern rockets he had been hearing about from the Commodore and the other captains. A patch of passenger pigeon dropping remained on the deck, missed by the moppers, and he fixated on it as Stephen continued.

"The next recorded use of rockets in warfare was on the Iberian Peninsula in 1249, used by the Arabs, and sweet Valencia was attacked by the most dreadful rockets in 1288," Stephen droned. "Although, of course, there are no details of the construction of the early rockets, I would guess the tubular rocket cases were probably made of layers of tightly wrapped paper, coated with shellac. For the propulsion, I would suppose they used the most basic black powder mixture of ground charcoal, saltpetre, and sulfur. Even England's own dear Roger Bacon wrote formulae for gunpowder, as far back as 1248, in *Epistola*. As you well know, India has used rockets against our country most effectively; Tippu Sultan, the son of Hyder Ali, used rockets against us at Seringapatam."

Jack's eyes glazed over, as his horse's eyes had done the day of his last ride, perhaps from similar cause. He gazed around in desperation; a snake chose that moment to slither across his holy quarterdeck. Stephen smiled lovingly upon it as he spoke: it was the *crotalida sistrurus*, the sweet *crotalus horridus atricaudatus* variety, and he loved it dearly. Jack Audibly longed to stomp the brute under his polished boots, but it was one of Stephen's American species, so he dared not tread on it. His teeth gritted of themselves; he was no sea lawyer, but he wondered about the ramifications should he inflict some minor physical injury to the snake; would it then fall under legitimate cappabarre should the purser be suggested to take the damaged goods for his mess?

"I believe the rockets we use today, Sir Congreve's model, have metal loops into which a guide stick can be inserted and crimped,"

Stephen continued. "They can be launched either from ladders or horizontally along the ground. That's what we used in Boulogne, at least, and as well you know, it is what we used when we burned Copenhagen; we used hundreds of rockets there—a most admirable weapon, if you care for destruction."

Stephen paused for breath. Jack paused for lunch. He had heard all he wanted to hear from Stephen, who could be an infernal windbag when asked the simplest question.

The Americans were getting rambunctious—there was no question of it. Their attitude towards England wanted improvement; they were impolite to the seamen when they spotted them in town, and their behaviours were uncalled for, to say the least. As *Aghast* plied the shores east of the Chesapeake Bay, near the inlet of the Miles River, Audibly spotted a crudely constructed Royal Navy "Foodfight" signal flag being hoisted over a residence in Saint Michaels when the *Aghast* came into view. Not wanting to attack civilians, but determined to avenge the insult, he ordered his men to overshoot the town, high enough to avoid casualties; only the house on Mulberry Street bearing the pennant was struck, and the only injury was to a rooster, whose leg was broken by a cannonball. The American chronicles made no mention of the incident at the time, but perhaps it instilled a sense of dignity into the proceedings, as Captain Audibly did not see any more "Foodfight" signals after that incident.

The sun rose earlier each day, temperatures rose; the summer solstice came and went. The planned invasion of Washington was nearing. Following Napoleon's defeat, thousands of veteran British soldiers had become available for service in America, and troopships were arriving daily. More and more British ships arrived and took up station, and Jack Audibly was engaged in increasing social intercourse with his colleagues, but still precious little action.

As they had opined, Stephen's assignment in Maryland was untenable. When the attack plans were finalized, Jack summoned him back to the *Aghast* from his activities, official, unofficial, and scientific, and all shoregoing leave was halted, including the raids on the farms. The war became more imminent; tension filled the air.

In August, when England took the town of Bladensburg, Maryland, Jack finally got to see the rockets in action; they had turned the flank of the American troops defencing Washington, D.C., *Aghast* playing only the most peripheral supporting role, taking no American ships in prize but helping to fire on and sink three ships. Jack heard with chagrin that rowdy British troops under orders from Admiral Sir George Cockburn had set fire to Washington, burning the Capitol (including the three thousand volume library), the President's House, and the Navy Arsenal, more from frustration at the course of the war and anger at the burning of York, Canada than from strategic value. Jack visualized the mad scramble—trying to find strategic papers in the burning buildings before they went up in flame—the dismay of the Americans at seeing their fledgling capital city senselessly destroyed. Washington, D.C. was not a particularly popular capital city—even the Americans referred to it as "a mud-hole equal to the Great Serbonian Bog"—but arson was shameful nonetheless. Jack was further chagrined that the British troops had failed to capture the design drawings for the *U.S.S. Constitution*, which apparently went up in the flames—Stephen had given him some intelligence about what he called "diagonal riders," but had not the technical cognizance to describe well the innovation. He was not particularly concerned about the Capitol building; it couldn't have been much of a loss, he thought, having been designed by an Irishman, James Hoban—like as not the man had never suffered to wear shoes—the sot—but Jack still regretted unnecessary destructiveness in any case. Cockburn tried to claim that it was the Colonists themselves that had burnt the Navy Yard, an unlikely tale, to be sure. Cockburn had been looting, in addition, and it was known that he had personally stolen a wooden medicine chest he favoured, President Madison's personal, bound copy of U.S. government receipts and expenditures, and a black-bound family Bible belonging to Dorothea Payne Madison, the President's wife, along with her certificate of marriage which had been tucked inside it, merely as a souvenir; a court-martial offense. Jack had no use for Admiral Cockburn—the brute had disgraced the Union Jack the previous year at Hampton, Virginia, indulging his troops in an orgy of violence; rape, arson, and looting, and would be a fool and an embarrassment wherever he posted. Clearly, there had been no improvement since Cockburn's syphilitic eponymous progenitor. Jack hoped he would not be called upon to serve under the man. He would obey direct commands if he could unmistakably see the signals, but Cockburn was not an officer to be respected.

Jack's spirits flagged uncharacteristically; he took no elation or glee from the floggings of his men; Stephen's species were underfoot at best; his latest mail from Sophie reported that Georges had eaten an excess of blood sausages and had had a week-long bellyache; the roof leaked at the slightest drizzle; Fancy and Carlotta were beginning to take a new notice of boys, and had begun blushing their cheeks and lampblacking their eyebrows; the children's mathematics tutor had quit, he'd been the third one that month; Captain Adeane who lived behind Colton sent his kindly regards, he was such a dear man to have come visiting numerous times to see to the roof, but although his tools were splendid, the roof still leaked; poor, sweet Parson Hinksey had returned, his wife, Lucy Smith Hinksey had died in Bombay of an unmentionable disease, how she had caught it was unimaginable, and Sophie was trying in every possible way to comfort the dear man of his loss, but he was inconsolably desolate and lonely, although she visited with him as often as ever she could; the little girls had taken to cursing again, and she had not the faintest idea what could have brought it on; for the good news, Fancy and Carlotta had quite improved their penmanship, and that sweet Mr. Blabbington of Jack's command was kind enough to correspond with them; and at least her mother, Mrs. Williams, was enjoying the best of health and spirits, and was even so robust as to project to sort out Jack's over-cluttered oversized storage chest for him within the fortnight, as he had often complained that he could not find anything in it; but she, Sophie, was afflicted with headaches every night, and even the act of writing this letter had provoked yet another, so she would sign off now, with some affection. Jack felt low, and his spirits did not lift at the sound of a returning libertyman, probably Mr. Mjollnir, loudly humming *The Hornet and the Peacock* overhead.

Stephen, too, had received mail from home, and was writhing and snarling in Irish. There was also a sheaf of paper in Stephen's packet which Bridget desired him to show to Captain Audibly for his opinion on it. Stephen asked Jack to look it over when he had the time. Jack glanced at it. It was difficult to read, in Bridget's childlike scrawl, but he made out that it was an attempted proof of why x^3 plus y^3 would never equal z^3. He studied it for a few moments, and then returned to rereading his own letter from Sophie. Later, he would dash a note to Bridget, telling her that it was a charming note she had sent him, and that she should indeed write to him again, perhaps taking care the next time to have fewer blots and erasures and smudges, but a charming little note it was, indeed.

Stephen did not volunteer the contents of his letter, other than a brief citation of a fragment from Hipponax, from 520 B.C.: "There are two days when a woman is a pleasure: the day one marries her and the day one buries her." Jack steered well clear of him, and pitied Mr. Playce, who was due to have a tooth pulled shortly. Playce had already reported to the sick-berth and was by now rollicking drunk; yet Jack cringed as he saw the doctor heading down, Stephen's own teeth clenched, the crumpled letter already smudged by the blood dripping from his palms. Jack recoiled when he heard the cannonfire; Stephen had deafened several crewmen in the process of removing their teeth. In truth, although he had never mentioned it aloud to the captain, for deafening, amazing, stupefying his patients, Stephen preferred to pull teeth in the dead of night, just above the cabin of his snoring captain - cannonfire weren't in it; but it would not serve today with Mr. Playce. Meanwhile, Jack Audibly thought grimly to the time, not funny then nor now, when he had been in the very act of deflowering a maiden, and Stephen had in good conscience snuck up to the window of their chamber and, in an effort to induce a partial, temporary insensibility and to abate what he believed would be her pain, had shot off one of his infernal tooth-pulling cannons, startling them both out of their inclination. He was glad now that Stephen had not been on board the night... was it Cathy?... Katie?... had visited him. Reverend Martinet started to ask Dr. Nattering about a numbness in his arms and a pressing, burning sensation he was experiencing in his chest. Nattering fairly growled at him without breaking stride, "take two slimedraughts and call me in the morning."

The only other mail of note (aside from the usual advertisements and bills that pursued him wherever he sailed) was a short note from Admiral Cochrane, summoning him aboard the flagship *Surprise* at his earliest convenience, for urgent orders. It was with a heavy heart that Jack ordered a course set for the *Surprise*.

20

The rising sun was full in his face; his heart lifted as he held his unopened orders in his hands, because he was certain that this meant that they would be happily concluding this war; he would soon be sailing homeward to Sophie and his dear children. He could barely detect through the deck the slight swell under the hull. Bits of seaweed were drifting alongside the ship, together with the jellyfish which had become so numerous in these waters of late. The land breeze brought with the morning dew wafts of honeysuckle and meadow grass. High over the masts circled a pair of seagulls, wheeling, calling.

"Commodores Downie and Macdonough being otherwise occupied elsewhere, by Virtue of the Power and Authority to us given, you are hereby required and directed to take the ships named in the margin under your command, and to proceed with the utmost expedition off the port of Baltimore, Maryland, and there make your dispositions for taking possession of Fort McHenry and the City of Baltimore by a sudden and vigorous assault. Hereof nor you nor any of you may fail, as you will answer the contrary at your peril."

The ships named were a frigate, a cutter, the rocket ship *Erebus*, which could fire better than forty shells per hour, when Captain Bartholomew was inclined to follow orders, and two small gunboats. Not a very large force, Jack thought, but certainly enough for the simple task assigned him. His heart soared within him. Soon, his mission would be complete, the ruckus would finally be ended, and he would return with honour to his dear Sophie, to his Georges, to Fancy and Carlotta. A broadtail pendant! He had commanded small forces before, and would delight in hoisting his flag again. Other fleets would have other assignments in the operations area. He knew that *Volcano* would see action, and *Cockchafer,* as well as other frigates, including the brave *Hebrus,* and the *Naglfar,* carrying the scrub Cockburn's flag, transferred from the *Severn,* and several ships of the line, but he was absolutely certain that his own group would be decisive in the battle.

He could hardly wait to begin! He chivvied Baretta Blondin to the maximum speed in returning to the dear *Aghast,* and wasted no time at all in messaging the ships that would be under his command, summoning their captains. To his utter delight, the gunboats were armed with Sir Congreve's rockets; he would finally get to see them in action. His would not be the only fleet at Ft. McHenry, of course, but he was determined that his would be the best. Victory was within his grasp!

He laid out his battle lines with biscuits and bowls; there were not enough ships in his command, nor did he expect many in opposition, to warrant many biscuits or bowls; he ate a few biscuits while he worried over the actions. He hoped he would have leisure enough after the little action to do a little mopping up on the lighthouse at Havre de Grace, and the miserable Irishman John O'Neill. The action at Fort McHenry would primarily fall to the British army, and the navy's unaccustomed role would be in support of the land action. He knew the army would somehow manage to make a complete cock-up of it, but he knew also that the Royal Navy would triumph, and he daydreamed of a great single-handed action, like Nelson's. Unthinkingly, he ate too many of the biscuits to finish his plans, but it mattered little—he called for his signalman.

"Hoist this message to the ships under my command: 'I am confident of success'."

The signalman hesitated. "The 'confident' flag still has pepperoni stains on it, which we are unable to remove. May I say, 'I expect success'?"

Jack sighed. "Make it so."

He spoke with Stephen briefly, making the customary arrangements before battle, handing him documents, although without the usual air of premonition; Baltimore would fall easily, perhaps ending the war. They discussed the nature of battle from

189

the point of view of philosophy. Stephen mentioned a very ambitious piece he had recently read called *The Sea-Officer's Tragedy*, which ended in disaster. They both agreed, however, that although any hack author can kill off the main character of his opera, a true artist may bring about a happier ending without distortion of reality. How much happier the story of Nelson would have been had he come, one day or other, laughing home as promised, to the dignified retirement from the busy scenes of life with honour he so richly deserved; how much more satisfied his fans would have been with such a conclusion to a long and distinguished service. If novels were closer to truth, however; the truth about mere mortals is that for so many of us, it's not our mortality that is so poignant, but that things go on, and on and on. There is no easy escape as there is in novels with clean endings; there are seldom clean conclusions. For every Nelson shot down in a classical moment of glory, there are scores of captains who come home time and again to the squalor of babies, their own and unknown; mumps, teething, tax collectors, frowsty in-laws, leaking roofs, eternal 'web-server down' messages, wives grown shrewish, old friends dozing through the retelling of major battles won, projectors, summer re-runs, teachers, incompetent professionals, thrill-seeking dentists, telemarketers calling at dinnertime, lawyers, ignorant gawkers, and the aches and pains of the slings and arrows. Tragedy need not end in disaster; tragedy ends in truth. Tragedy is not Beethoven's *Fifth Symphony*; tragedy is Ravel's *Bolero*.

Despite his embarrassment over the soiled signal flag, he was filled to the brim with the very greatest elation, darts of joy shooting from his heart, as he triumphantly sailed toward Fort McHenry, soon to be the site of his greatest victory! What joy, what unalloyed joy, to be instrumental in the conquering reunification of the Empire!

THE END